INTERCULTURAL CITY

SERIES: BOOK 2

Planning for the Intercultural City

Jude Bloomfield & Franco Bianchini

D1428210

First published in the UK in 2004 by Comedia
Copyright © 2004 edited by Phil Wood
A catalogue record of this book is available from the British Library

ISBN 1-873667-92-2

Comedia
The Round, Bournes Green
Stroud, GL6 7NL
www.comedia.org.uk

Book design and photography:
Brecknock Consulting
www.brecknockconsulting.com.au

Printed and bound by:
Pims Digital
11-14 Repton Close
Burnt Mills
Basildon
Essex SS13 1LJ
jstannard@pims.co.uk
+44 (01268) 530100

This and other Comedia publications available through
Eco-Distribution
Crosswell, Eglywswrw
Pembrokeshire, SA41 3TE
jill.chandler@virgin.net
+44 (01239) 891431

Contents

Acknowledgements

The authors would like to thank all the informants who gave interviews, discussing and showing us round their projects.

We would also like to express our thanks to Andy Howell and colleagues from Birmingham City Council Policy Division and Comedia for commissioning a joint report: "Planning for the Cosmopolitan City" (January 2002, unpublished) on best practice in intercultural urban policy initiatives in Europe and abroad on which the book is based. We would also like to thank Charles Landry for his editorial advice.

In addition Jude Bloomfield would like to express gratitude to MaryAnn De Vlieg of IETM for commissioning the report on multicultural and intercultural performing arts in Europe, *Crossing the Rainbow*, (www.ietm.org – October, 2003) from which much of the research in Part II is drawn.

The book has been written collaboratively by the two authors except for Part I whose sole author was Jude Bloomfield.

Setting
the Scene

There has been in recent years in the UK a lively debate on the future of the British approach to managing ethnic and cultural diversity, which in this book we describe as 'corporate multiculturalism'.

An example is the debate started by David Goodhart's article in *Prospect* (Goodhart, 2004), which presumes an inherent conflict between solidarity and diversity, arguing that systems which experience the shock of change – including demographic transformations due to immigration - inevitably have difficulties of absorption.

The debate on the future of multiculturalism in Britain should be more closely related to that on the possible responses to globalization. The emergence of a globally competitive hub in the South East of England – supported by the Government's economic strategy - is undermining the potential of regional clusters, which could build on the potential of interculturalism as a force for economic innovation. The heightening of the North-South divide in Britain is acting to reinforce xenophobia. There could, however, be an alternative, municipal and regionalist, approach to globalisation, building on cultural diversity as a resource for economic and urban regeneration.

Many people in the UK and elsewhere see the process of economic globalisation as a threat to local distinctiveness and identity. Globalisation is a driving force behind the rediscovery of national, regional and local identities, as shown by phenomena like the growing popularity of the St. George's flag in England.

In the case of Scotland and Wales clear national identities can be discerned, including the two nations' Celtic heritage, a history of conflict with England and openness to continental European influences. The democratic political space and the distinctive national media in Scotland and Wales have allowed for the emergence of a separate public discourse, which is as likely to address collaboration with Catalonia or Emilia Romagna as with London.

In contrast, there is a risk of a defensive, rather than outgoing, revival of Englishness, in response to the redrawing of the boundaries of the nation state and to the decline of Britain's global position, in its limbo between being the 'junior partner' of the United States and a leader of a strengthened European Union.

Devolution re-negotiated the internal relationships within the British state for Scotland, Wales and Northern Ireland, through a partial redistribution of power. But the fact that it was not a federal redistribution meant that in England it was purely a bureaucratic decentralisation to the regions, without establishing democratically legitimate institutions, although there are proposals for Regional Assemblies. So while devolution produced a democratically legitimated new focus for Scottish, Welsh and Northern Irish identity, it only served to heighten the lack of decentralised democratic institutions in England and its regions.

The danger of a reinvoked Englishness which has no democratic underpinning is that it could seek to define English identity negatively, as what it is not, reinforcing xenophobic stereotypes and anti-European sentiments, or reasserting primordial, territorial claims to being the essential native English (a danger which is visible in political phenomena like the rise of UKIP and, to a lesser degree, of the BNP).

We tend to forget that English history is shaped by hybridity and intercultural exchange. Take the example of Leicester and its county. The 2001 Census classed 36.1% of Leicester's population as "non-White". The corresponding percentages for England were 9.1%, and for the East Midlands region 6.5%. Leicester is expected to become, at some point during the second decade of this century, one the first cities in Europe where over 50% of the population will be "non-White". Leicester's multi-ethnic character is largely due to postwar immigration, mainly by Indians and Pakistanis who moved to the city from East Africa in the early 1970s, and from the Indian sub-continent. However, the city has been shaped by intercultural influences throughout its history.

The Roman name for Leicester was Ratae Coritanorum. Originally a Celtic settlement of the Coritani people, it became after the Roman invasion of Britain a *civitas* capital, a second rank town in the country's new three-level urban hierarchy. The Romans brought a mixture of people from their empire, including most probably Africans and Syrians. After the fall of the Roman empire Leicester's identity was reshaped by the Saxons from Northern Germany. St. Nicholas, a beautiful Saxon church, still stands in the city centre, probably built on the foundations of a Roman temple. It incorporates Roman pillars and is adjacent to the impressive ruins of the Roman baths. After the Viking invasions the city was incorporated in that part of England known as the Danelaw. Danish influences remain in the names of villages on the city's outskirts like Groby, Ratby and Frisby ("by" meaning "town" in Danish), and in the word *gatan* ("street" in Danish) incorporated in street names in Leicester city centre like Gallowtree Gate, Churchgate or Humberstone Gate.

The Norman conquest, lastly, brought French influences in the names of places and institutions, like Belvoir Street in the city centre or Belvoir Castle in the county, the town of Ashby de la Zouch and De Montfort University itself (named after 13th century warlord and politician Simon De Montfort). Such an intercultural history is true of most towns and cities.

There are today real anxieties among white lower middle class and middle class people also in the more affluent parts of Britain about work security and employment, in an economy which is increasingly exposed to fierce global competition. These fears, however, need to be addressed by social measures designed to cushion the worst effects of economic globalisation, while countering racial stereotypes and scape-goating. The BNP is targetting embattled social groups in areas of electoral apathy and abstention, such as white working class people in declining northern mill towns or marginal rural areas and Cornish fishing ports. Anti-European propaganda is being used in the fishing ports and anti-immigration rhetoric in areas like the mill towns where there are ethnic minority communities.

We recognise, however, that the aftermath of 9/11 has made the advocacy of intercultural approaches more difficult, with the increasing infringement of civil liberties produced by the "war on terror". The rise of Islamophobia is especially troubling. It manifests itself in some cases in the group identification of Islam with its fundamendalist political form, and in the demonisation of Muslims as a whole as responsible for terrorist acts.

We agree with those who argue that we need to re-examine multiculturalism as a paradigm, but where we differ is in the causes of its failure and the remedy. The key reason for the relative failure of multiculturalism is that it has inhibited intercultural mixing and understanding, sharing and exchange in the public sphere. If we do not have such an intercultural understanding, any policy of integration will fail. The nature of the public domain has to be re-negotiated and the public culture re-imagined in an intercultural light.

Without such transformation, the idea of integrating into 'Britishness' advocated by Trevor Phillips (2004a and 2004b), would be an integration into a pre-constituted national identity with which many citizens do not identify and have no hand in defining. Furthermore, such conceptions of Britishness, outside of a negotiated open dialogue about the nature and principles of the civic culture, would leave untouched the self-flattering imperial national narrative which has been in crisis for so long. An intercultural approach should rather build on certain characteristics of Britishness such as its acceptance of multiple identities, openness and cosmopolitanism.

Without such re-founding of national narratives and national institutions, there is a danger of falling back on the traditional and the parochial, emphasising indigenous roots rather than a more cosmopolitan sense of national unity that draws upon "an open sense of place" and a politics of engagement with multiple identities and cosmopolitan affiliations. (Amin, Massey and Thrift, 2003, 37)

In short, an intercultural recasting of both Englishness and Britishness is required.

Part of an intercultural approach is to resist the temptation of laying the blame for racism and xenophobia mainly on marginalised social groups like the white working class in declining industrial towns. It is also to recognise that there are problems of mutual ignorance and of generalising on the basis of little or no knowledge, which are widespread and not the preserve of one particular social group. What is important in an intercultural mentality is that rather than sticking to our ignorance and justifying our prejudices, we recognise the need to find out and get to know the other. Intercultural exchange and curiosity should lead to a process of mutual discovery and learning between all the different cultural and ethnic groups which make up the population.

The starting premise for adopting an intercultural approach is that multiculturalism in Britain has often failed to create the conditions for genuine communication, and that this has been damaging for all groups. Equally important, though, is that intercultural exchange should involve the different regions and nations within Britain, as well as our European neighbours and people from other continents whose difference may not be immediately visible because of their skin colour. While it is true that visible minorities generally suffer from greater discrimination and disadvantage, many white immigrants (for example, the Irish and Jews in the past, Albanians and Kosovans today) have experienced and are experiencing severe difficulties. There is a need, for example, for stronger policies to encourage more people to learn foreign languages and reverse the decline of language teaching in schools and universities. It would also be important to achieve a more balanced and optimistic view of the opportunities membership of the EU offers for education, training and exchanges of professional knowledge, going beyond the relatively popular but one-sided view that other EU member states have more to learn from the British model than vice versa.

This book argues that citizenship is the connective tissue of intercultural planning. By this we mean not only equality of opportunity, but also critical respect for other cultures, reflecting the cultural diversity of the city fully in public policy, public space and institutions. This means that we do not counterpose recognition of cultural difference to equality but see them as interdependent. This has become more vital since class has come to be seen as defined by ethnicity, and so many inequalities which derive from low-paid manual labour or routine service work, poor housing and schooling are seen in terms of ethnic stigma, rather than class.

The intercultural approach advocated in this book offers an alternative. Interculturalism goes beyond equal opportunities and respect for existing cultural differences, to the pluralist transformation of public space, institutions and civic culture. So it does not recognise cultural boundaries as fixed but as in a state of flux and remaking. An intercultural approach aims to facilitate dialogue, exchange and reciprocal understanding between people of different cultural backgrounds. Cities need to develop policies which prioritise funding for projects where different cultures intersect, 'contaminate' each other and hybridise. This contrasts with the multicultural model, where funding is directed within the well-defined boundaries of recognised cultural communities. In other words, city governments should promote cross-fertilisation across all cultural boundaries, between 'majority' and 'minorities', 'dominant' and 'sub' cultures, localities, classes, faiths, disciplines and genres, as the source of cultural, social, civic and economic innovation.

The book starts by putting forward the argument for the intercultural city, and by evaluating different approaches to dealing with cultural diversity. It then highlights problematic urban trends, including the needs to address socio-economic inequalities, the spatial segregation of ethnic minority groups and ethnic segregation in public life. It discusses the challenge of creating a cosmopolitan civic identity and culture, and offers exemplary intercultural initiatives, found in a variety of European cities and across a range of policy fields, from local economic development to health, education, place marketing and festivals. The concluding section focuses on the need to rethink the practices of city authorities. The aim is to make urban policy making processes more open to creative ideas, and better able to learn from the experiences of other cities, and to collaborate with the academic community and the third sector so that the richness of talent, expressiveness and entrepreneurship of ethnic minority groups can be realised and harnessed to the benefit of the city as a whole. The overall aim is to start a debate on the potential of an intercultural approach to transform our cities into culturally and economically vibrant and shared places for all citizens.

PART ONE

The Argument for the Intercultural City

The Dynamics of Migration in Europe

People are on the move, as immigrants, business visitors, tourists, asylum seekers. But cities are fixed places. The only way cities can move is mentally: through openness to change, by responding to the vision and imagination of their citizens, and through welcoming newcomers and conscripting their skills and talents to revitalise themselves. Most people do not move country unless they have to, through economic need, insecurity or persecution. And some move simply because they feel another city will allow them to fulfil their dreams of a better life as they value human rights more strongly, are more vibrant or offer opportunities.

The art of the cosmopolitan city is to harness the largely reluctant movement of newcomers, to stir itself up, to enlarge its horizons and make newcomers feel at home as citizens, as it makes tourists welcome as temporary citizens. This book aims to describe a trajectory for cities to become more cosmopolitan places that provide a secure, prosperous and productive future for immigrants, a safe haven and refuge for the persecuted, and create a vibrant culture and communication between citizens of all backgrounds.

Migration and the patterns of migrant settlement in major West European cities is not an accident. It was determined by policy. In the post-war period the demand for labour to fuel economic reconstruction in Western Europe was the major 'pull' factor in migration. Britain and France satisfied their needs by recruiting from their colonies or ex-colonies. It was state instigated, organised through state recruitment offices, such as the French ONI which evaluated the physical attributes, skills and 'suitability' of workers. Familiarity with the metropolitan language and family or communal migration chains also shaped the pattern of settlement. Even in the case of the comparatively free market Britain, the Ministries of Health and Transport actively advertised for labour in the West Indies and sub-Continent. Immigrants staffed the public services – as drivers and conductors on buses and trains and auxiliaries, nurses and doctors in the health service. Most found work in semi-skilled jobs in factories where they were part of the mass market of consumer goods they produced. These immigrants became citizens as part of a prior colonial deal, although Algerians migrating to France after independence in 1962, could only enter as foreign nationals.

By 1973-74 as workers' protest at the low level of wages and lack of control in the workplace had begun to bite and the first oil crisis set in, all the former imperial countries put a stop to primary immigration and began to impose restrictions on right of entry even where, as in the case of British Commonwealth citizens, the newcomers had passports. They were forced to queue and their rights were curtailed but under pressure of international law, generally family reunion was allowed to go ahead. These immigrants were the first generation - Maghrebin, African Caribbean and Asian citizens of the metropolitan powers.

A second system of labour recruitment grew up outside of ex-colonial citizenship migration. Germany established a guest worker system, by recruiting cheap labour from the rural underdeveloped periphery of Europe for the expanding industries of Germany's post-war economic reconstruction. They signed inter-state agreements with Italy, Turkey, Greece, Spain and Yugoslavia, Austria, Switzerland, Belgium and the Netherlands followed variants of this system. Rather than being offered hospitality as 'guests', they were denied rights of settlement and naturalisation, but continued to stay, renewing their yearly contracts as it was in employers' interests to have continuity in the workforce. Despite the German stop on recruitment at the same time as the other West European powers, family reunion continued to take place under international law. This produced the German, Austrian and Swiss anomaly of long-term settlement, particularly of Turks, without citizenship rights, whereas in Belgium and the Netherlands, guestworkers' status was gradually equalized.

After a long fiercely contested internal struggle and debate citizenship and nationality laws have finally been revised to confer German citizenship after a period of eight years residence for 'guests' and automatic citizenship if born on the territory (*ius soli*) and to allow dual German/Turkish nationality. The cultural distance between Germans and Turks was wider than between the metropolis and the colonised as in Britain or France, partly because there was no imposed common language or education system, and partly because the German state made no provision for language learning and integration for many years. Recruited from the uneducated rural poor, factory work reinforced their low economic status. This was compounded by an inferior education and training for their children which has led to 're-ethnicisation' – a going back to roots. Young men more frequently are being sent to Turkey to find wives rather than mix with third generation German Turkish girls and there is a new emphasis on orthodox Islamic practices.

The guestworker system has become *de facto* a contemporary model of immigration, where short-term, casual, and cash-in-hand work in the informal economy leads to longer term settlement of undocumented workers, who have no rights, insurance or legal protection. This gives *carte blanche* to employers to exploit workers by plugging gaps in the labour market by filling unpalatable, low-paid jobs. It also gives huge discretionary power to the state to prove its tough stand periodically using clandestine migrants as whipping boys for a country's social problems and discontents. The exemplary removals or highly publicised tightening of controls are examples as occurred in France when Charles Pasqua was Minister of the Interior or as happened in Spain under Aznar. The media has connived with populist politicians and governments in exclusively (mis) representing immigrants as scroungers, criminals, drug addicts and Islamic terrorists, to enlist reactionary support in their circulation wars.

Since the 1980s migration measured by the number of foreign born people without citizenship began to exceed population growth. (Stalker, 2001,15) Globalisation is accelerating the pace of this migration and changing its composition through creating an informal economy. The powerful new 'pull' factors drawing people to Western Europe are not officially acknowledged. The new global information economy with deregulated markets, the dominance of financial and information services, combined with demographic decline and the demise of statutory social entitlements, has produced sharply divided global cities with new 'leisured' and service classes. They are composed, on the one hand, of 'symbolic analysts', consultants and managers in financial services, IT and the entertainment industries, and on the other, private catering and care services for the new middle classes. (Sassen, Portes, Kalb et.al, 2000)

There is also a new tertiary working class in call centres, contract cleaning, security and maintenance firms. The demand for these services and those who carry them out, has risen exponentially with the growth of the globalised economy. So the demand for cheap labour, which tends to be undocumented workers has grown despite state protestations and policies to the contrary. According to Alejandro Portes, this is an unstoppable fact of life. The pull factor is the demand in advanced post-industrial economies on the one hand. To fill niche scarcities such as nurses and engineers and on the other, it draws in workers for low-paid jobs which the domestic workforce refuses to undertake. (Portes, 1997) This latter demand sucks in and preys off clandestine migrants and the system contrives to worsen their civic and social status and maximise their insecurity. Cosmopolitan cities will have to address their lack of rights and visibility by affirming their presence and offering support to advance their welfare, self-organisation and social integration. Rome City Council, for example, has implemented a scheme to pay the tax imposed on domestics to regularise their status and to pay the tuition fees for them to train as registered and qualified child-minders.

'Push' factors exist as well, precipitated by the global economic and environmental crisis and the break up of the old world order, which are leading to the mounting displacement of people. The growth of asylum-seeking has been largely absorbed in Third World neighbouring countries. Already in 1991 the UNHCR estimated that of the 14-16 million refugees in the world 11 million were absorbed in Africa, Asia and the Near East, 1 million in the United States and 700,000 in Europe. (CLRAE, 1992). That is only 6%. Economic marginalisation – especially of Africa, the demise of the Soviet empire and ethnic war mean that asylum seekers, often well-educated but poor, arrive desperate and traumatised. If they make it to Europe, they face a new fortress regime designed increasingly to exclude them or make life tough and they have already suffered more than most. Our cities in Europe claiming to be liberal in the future will be challenged to prove how universalist and open they are, by acting as 'cities of refuge' (Derrida, 2000) for displaced and stateless people to realise their possibilities. The Scottish Carnival of Arts, described later, gives a glimpse of the potential if asylum seekers are valued as people with skills and cultural know-how to contribute, which can be channelled into collective self-help, creative artistic projects, social regeneration and further along the line an economic contribution.

These trends are changing the ethnic composition and demography of the big cities so they are becoming more culturally diverse, to the point where ethnic minorities are projected to form the majority in Leicester by 2010. Ethnic minorities form a growing and youthful component of such cities – in Birmingham 21% in the 1991 census and 30% in the latest census. As a result of a higher birth rate among British Asians, the ethnic minority population forms over a third of the 0-17 year age group, with particularly strong Pakistani presence among young people (16.4%). The profile of Birmingham also shows a growth of inter-ethnic partnerships, especially between African

Caribbean men and white women, and thus, of mixed identities, and growing religious diversity. (Birmingham Stephen Lawrence Inquiry Commission, 2001, 13 and 22) The expansion of the European Union will further increase this ethnic mix, although as they are 'seen' as white it will be less visible.

How cities respond to these demographic and cultural changes will determine their futures. If they close in it will lead to fragmented, conflict ridden, ghettoised settlements, which under-explores and under-exploits potential. If they are welcomed it can become a source of strength and creative infusion making cities more dynamic and adaptive. (Amendola, 1998, 83-84) Cities have begun to see cultural diversity as an asset and opportunity, rather than a problem or threat, but thinking this through and acting consistently and imaginatively in all spheres of urban life will necessitate a deeper shift in mindset, in local and national government, in the media and public institutions and in the wider society.

The varied waves of migration have extended the boundaries of West European cities beyond their physical confines, linking them in history, economic flows and cultural influences to the immigrants' countries of origins. This challenges cities to rethink their links with the outside world, and develop new opportunities for economic and cultural exchange which are reciprocally beneficial and help to create more equal relationships. They include the developing diasporic economic networks with India, China, and others and the links entrepreneurs create for mutual benefit in business, finance and trade. A global economy needs the skills of the culturally diverse. So for cities, the cultural and educational potential of international links become highly significant, giving young people, in particular, access to knowledge of another culture through direct exchanges, study and tourist visits, artistic tours and performances. For example, Birmingham City Council has a twinning relationship with Johannesburg, South Africa, part of which entailed IBM equipping Soweto schools with computer hardware and setting up Internet links with twenty Birmingham schools as well as a tour of the Soweto children's choir and links with Aston Villa football club. (see Birmingham City Council website) The scope for developing city international policies to connect diverse local civil societies – people to people, through schools, voluntary groups, local businesses, sports associations, the club scene to their counterparts abroad, is immense, but under-explored.

The discretionary power of the state that can scapegoat illegal and poor migrants, allied to media stereotyping, plays on public fear and insecurity, ignorance of 'the other', and the unknown. As real international political and economic uncertainty deriving from globalisation has increased, along with uncertainty about Britain's global role and post-imperial identity, so negative images of immigrants have grown and positive public images have diminished. (Alibhai-Brown, 1996; 1997) This gives a distorted, therefore, false picture of migration and cultural diversity, focussing only on numbers, illegality and difference as something threatening or dangerous. These contorted images of immigrants, ethnic minority groups and individuals pose a problem to cities. They undermine civic integration and so reduce the possibilities of creating positive social experiences of meeting and mixing with others. They restrict too the possibilities for cities to project positive counter images of cultural diversity and intercultural citizenship in the press, in public debate, and policy discussion, in its publicity, marketing and tourist promotion. These are pre-conditions for cultural diversity to become highly prized and to able to build positive attachment to the city as a centre of civic engagement, cultural and social interaction and creative innovation.

Cities now operate in a more complex national and international system and respond to forces beyond the nation state. They face more diverse sources of command, directives and authority than before – including from the regions in most of Europe, the European Union, international monetary institutions and regulatory bodies. (Borja and Castells, 1996; Le Galès, 2003) This does not amount to the demise of the nation state but to competing sources of power and pressure, but also of resources. It offers new opportunities which depend far more on the capacity of cities to act strategically, to make alliances and networks for mutual benefit and counter zero-sum-game competition, to assert their autonomy as actors on the world stage. However, the huge pressures of international competitiveness and inter-urban hierarchy should not be underestimated, but nor should they be allowed to dictate unchallenged.

This new political stage calls for governance rather than government by cities, based on local growth coalitions of civil society and 'the third sector'. Only by mobilising local business and the voluntary sector can the needs of the local society be given strategic priority over the international economy. Where service provision is no longer statutory, underwritten by the nation state, service delivery relies on the mobilisation of self-organised communities and interests -

environmental groups, ethnic minorities, women and the disabled to shape services to their needs. (Mayo, 1992) This requires politicians become not only well-networked, open and media-friendly entrepreneurial managers, but at the same time develop a strategic vision through sharing power with the diverse public, recognising the breadth of coalitions, and the inclusiveness of civic networks will determine how resilient and autonomous the city can be.

The World in Your City

Cultural diversity, when positively presented, celebrates difference. Too often in political discourse, media representations and popular perception it is talked about as a problem. We claim it as an intrinsic value parallel to biodiversity, that can endow the whole city and society with riches which can enhance the quality of all our lives. In this sense multicultural and intercultural arguments coincide. Yet in emphasising difference the intrinsic value of a culture has been lost sight of. Not because it is different *per se*, but because it embodies a way of life and system of meaning. (Tomlinson, 1999, 68) A culture is a way of thinking and understanding the cosmos, the environment and a specific society and materially embodies that understanding especially through art, artefacts and practices. Together cultures form the multiplicity of human experience which contribute different ways of making sense of existence and alternative ways of doing and seeing that can add new perspectives, visions, sounds, senses and values to society as a whole.

Diversity does not necessarily mean that cultures are at odds or in conflict. They can have a non-antagonistic relationship and be complementary, because core dimensions of their idiom are translatable across other cultures, divided by space and even by long periods of time. So they are not 'incommensurable' as some philosophers claim, and only comprehensible to those brought up in the culture or adherents of it. So instead you can be British and attached to France, French language, literature, intellectual life, countryside and cuisine. You can be secular and Jewish, a non-believer who is moved by choral music and Russian icon painting, a Muslim who performs rap.

Public argument about cultural diversity has been underpinned for a long time by defensiveness, based on racial fears of numbers of immigrants, of being 'swamped' by aliens and a fantasy 'threshold of tolerance' being exceeded. Multicultural reality is a fact. The policy imperative is to turn it to the advantage of cities and society as a whole, to challenge the negative portrayal of immigrants as an economic, social or cultural threat and to counter racist institutional practices and perceptions. (Alibhai-Brown, 2000)

Where images are positive, they tend largely towards exotic stereotypes, such as African-Caribbeans being good at sport and music, implying they are by definition no good at intellectual or professional pursuits. Their social contribution to public services like transport and health and to care services is undervalued, and does not counterbalance the stereotype. Again Asian contributions to professions like engineering, law, accountancy and IT do not play a major role in newspaper representations, whereas ethnic shops and restaurants do. There is very little knowledge or coverage of ethnic minority business, banks and entrepreneurship and how they have contributed to the economy as a whole and the regeneration of the inner city, in particular, especially as the recent Home Office report concluded that immigration makes a net contribution of £2.6 billion to the economy. Even as today there is a crisis of rural post-offices and threats of closure, no connection has been made with how urban sub-post-offices and corner shops were saved in the 1970s and 1980s by the entrepreneurial commitment of Ugandan and Kenyan Asian immigrants. We take for granted cultural hybrids in cuisine, textiles, fashion production and design, rock and dance music, hip hop theatre and film, Bollywood, musical reviews, stand-up comedy, photography and photo journalism. The dynamism that these cross-over and fusion forms have produced in the commercial sector can be tapped throughout industry, in other art forms, in IT and communications, education and civic life so that cultural mixing leads to new ways of thinking, imagining and experimenting.

The promotion of cultural diversity as a positive public good has to show how it benefits the whole society through cultural renewal and innovation. This case is rarely made for cultural diversity. Critics such as Kenan Malik argue that cultural diversity has no intrinsic value, that it is only "important because it allows us to compare and contrast different values, beliefs and lifestyles, make judgements upon them, and decide which are better and which worse. It is important, in other words, because it allows us to engage in political dialogue and debate that can help create more universal values and beliefs". (Malik, 2002) While public debate and cultural criticism are themselves part of a universalistic framework within which aims can be agreed, they are also essential for airing disagreements and agreeing to differ. Any consensus that is arrived at in a diverse and democratic society can only be political, not cultural. At most the consensus around culture will be based on shared elements of all cultures, but that does not mean that people will give up their different beliefs or practices and become uniform, public citizens.

Cultures are complex systems of assessing importance and generating meaning. They are dynamic and not fixed. They may involve a language and literature, a national landscape or a religion as the key symbols and practices that define it. Culture cannot be reduced to a set of political values with which you agree or disagree. For example, how can you disagree with another language or art form that stems from a particular experience even if I, personally, do not know or understand it? To deny the value of the diversity of languages and imaginative life forms embodied in the cultures of others, is to presume the inherent superiority of your own culture. This is based on historical blindness, since all cultures develop through contact with and selective absorption of outside influences. Such a view presumes cultures are fixed wholes to be judged and rejected, or wholly accepted, rather than engaged with in their complexity, with partial modifications, selective borrowings and cross-fertilisation.

To arrive at a political consensus on certain universalist values does not require people to give up all their beliefs and cultural practices. Instead it involves finding common ground and a framework for co-existence and shared experience as a political community. Within that framework, those practices which infringe the rights of others or individual rights of minority members are curtailed by law or modified through negotiated agreement. Cultural diversity requires an ethic of respect on all sides, combined with open criticism and debate of differences, to arrive at any universal values or even more limited procedural agreements.

Secularism does not mean that people give up their faith or renounce the beliefs they hold dear, but it may entail them modifying their form or expression in the public domain. Secularism is not a belief system like atheism or agnosticism but an approach governing the relationship between state and religion, as a relationship of public and private. Therefore, secularism requires that religion be voluntary and communal, based on private choice and free association. So the state cannot enforce a religion on the public or favour one religion over others, but should deal equally with citizens regardless of their religious belonging or lack of faith. It also has implications for practising believers in religious associations that they do not impose their beliefs forcibly on others.

The interpretation given to 'laicité ' – secularism - in France at the present time that students cannot wear a large cross, skull cap or headscarf in school is hostile to pluralism and discriminatory in its effects, prejudicing the education of Muslim girls, in particular, at whom the law is really aimed. This interpretation of secularism mistakes personal symbols of religious or cultural identity as signs of mental closure or proselytising intent. Yet the secularism of the state does not mean society is not pluralist, so that when private citizens of diverse backgrounds and faiths enter public space, they stop being who they are and become abstractly uniform. On the contrary, secularism is a response to managing diversity of belief so that it does not disintegrate into violent conflict as happened in the religious wars of the 16th and 17th Centuries. In a democratic society, the rules of public institutions have to be rewritten in accord with the more diverse society they are there to serve.

We are far from that situation in Britain with an established Church of England, bishops in the House of Lords, religious education in state schools and the promotion by government of separate, state-funded, selective denominational schools. In addition, laws outlawing discrimination on racial or ethnic grounds exclude discrimination on religious grounds. Secularism, if applied consistently, entails a separation of Church and state, mixed state schools where comparative religion is taught with the same degree of dispassionate curiosity as history or philosophy. It would also mean equal protection under the law whatever one's race, religion or broader ethnicity. In other words, the citizenry is plural and diverse, the state should act with impartiality in the face of those diverse cultural characteristics and beliefs in the public domain. In civil society, ideas and beliefs should be freely practised (within the limits of democratic bounds and respect for others) and openly contested through public debate and cultural expression in the media and other public forums.

This is not an argument for propping up the traditional aspects of cultures. The bearers and practitioners of the culture are responsible for its continuation and renewal. They have to believe in its worth, organise to reproduce and develop the culture, applying for state protection where appropriate, support for infrastructure or projects where they have to justify the value of the intervention to the whole society. For example, the main Turkish organisation of mosques in the Netherlands, the Diyanet, has applied to the Dutch government for authorisation to train imams in the Netherlands who will be Dutch mother tongue, circumventing the need to import imams from Turkey, and enabling the mosques to appeal to the younger generation of Dutch-speaking Turks. It is in their interest to renew their religious institutions by making the language of the liturgy vernacular. They would also become a religious institution more adapted to Dutch society –a hybrid 'Euro-Islam'. Equally, it is in the interest of Dutch society to allow the same rights of religious association, internally regulated education and training to Muslims as to other religious denominations and to foster such cultural adaptation.

Cultural recognition has its own importance, but to realise the full benefits of cultural diversity, it must be linked to broader equal opportunities and eliminate racism embedded within institutions. As Susan Fainstein puts it: "An ethos of diversity cannot be developed separately from an understanding of the economic bases of inequality". (Fainstein, 1999, 259) Ethnic minorities locked in inner cities, on declining estates or unemployed without training or job opportunities cannot develop their talents and capabilities. Importantly the industries of culture, including communications and IT, have become the leading economic sector in post-industrial economies. If diverse cultural attributes, cannot be turned into assets of employment, self-employment and small business, then minority cultures will still not find their voice or audience beyond their own, and will be underrepresented within the culture as a whole. Minority cultures will remain stunted in terms of their potential for development and innovation, for creating cultural crossovers and in their capacity to influence mainstream, mass culture.

Cultural recognition has a material dimension, for example in the cultural field, such as how access to the grants system is organized; the availability of jobs in the cultural sector and elsewhere, culturally attuned training and small business support to help the independent sector expand, career progression and access to positions of management in mainstream cultural institutions. So cultural diversity cannot be counterposed to equality if the intersecting forms of inequality – social, economic, institutional/political and cultural are to be overcome. Urban policy has to address these inequalities at the same time, for example through targeted training, culturally sensitive local economic development and counter segregation strategies.

The city also has to concern itself with the collective self-organisation and representation of weakly organised or unrepresented interests. Yet many forms of political socialisation through local political parties and trade unions have declined. Employment is more fragmented, individualised and un-unionised. The voluntary sector has become more centralised and professionalised. Although local civic associations flourish, access to political and organisational resources for small, local groups, for those unfamiliar with the local political system and newcomers like refugees has become harder. Politics itself has changed with the demise of parts of statutory welfare provision, the development of local growth coalitions, environmental protest and lobbying groups, and growing media influence in the portrayal and shaping of issues. These all put the onus on the weak and oppressed, including ethnic minority groups, to organise collectively in their own interest, to develop wider strategic and inter-ethnic alliances in their campaigning, reshaping media representation and pressuring the formal political system.

Since associational life and a thriving, inclusive civil society is vital to a participatory democracy, if the city aims to achieve this, it has to counteract the tendencies to disenfranchisement and lack of voice of the poorest, weakest and most marginalised which include ethnic minorities among others such as parts of the white working class. Only through 'civic republicanism', where citizens actively organise and engage in local political debate and decision-making with the support of the city can political involvement be widened to outsiders and newcomers and political 'capital' be redistributed to redress this inequality. This would enhance the collective self-organisation, public presence and voice of minority groups.

The informants to the Cantle Report highlighted the lack of organisation within minority ethnic communities which prevented them from identifying and articulating their common concerns. (see Cantle Report, Appendix B, 58) They also complained of the difficulty for voluntary and community groups in accessing European Union funding to which they were entitled. (see Cantle Report, Appendix B, 57) So the city authorities should provide training in civic competencies that would enhance the collective representation of minority ethnic and other community groups and enable them to develop the strategic capacity for political intervention with a unified voice. Such competencies include understanding how the media works – especially in racial representation and framing of stories in a wider discourse, how to access the local media and gain favourable coverage and right of reply, how to campaign, network and apply for grants, and how to debate and formulate alternative policy. Such training can best be carried out by civic organisations acting as service providers as the Black Londoners' Forum does (see later) with the financial support of the city, showing its commitment to full and effective representation of minority ethnic citizens.

The Limits of Multiculturalism

Cultural recognition and respect allied to countering economic, social and political inequalities will not of itself overcome the limits of multiculturalism. Those problems are due to its tendency to reproduce separatism, to ossify and fix identities and communities as given and unchanging, and to marginalise them as 'minority', unconsciously reinforcing a dominant *ethnic* conception of the majority as white, rather than a *political* conception of a democratic 'majority'. All too often, official discourse refers to the 'white community' – which is a bogus racial characterisation of many different social and political interests and alignments. (see also Alibhai-Brown, 2000, ix) Indeed that 'white community' includes Irish, Italians, Greeks, Germans, Jews and Poles and a mix of cultures and languages. Because they appear white, we do not see their ethnicity. Perhaps the most serious defects of multiculturalism as a policy have been its failure to combat racial exclusion from public institutions, to reverse serious social inequality attributed to ethnicity and to counteract ethnic segregation.

One effect of emphasising respect for minority cultures and celebrating difference has been to leave most of the main public institutions untouched and unchallenged by the reality of a multicultural society. In the cultural institutions, for example, as in all other public institutions, black and minority ethnic faces are usually only seen backstage or serving in the kitchen and bars, not among the artistic directors or the boards of management. In terms of cultural financing, cultural diversity budgets are small and seen as an alternative to mainstream budgets for ethnic minority artists rather than as an additional source of funding to overcome exclusion. Likewise with programming, the stories and artistic forms derived from different cultural experience and traditions were, until recently, largely excluded from the mainstream repertoire, and still are in provincial and rural towns. Only too often they have exposure in studio and fringe venues, if at all. (Bloomfield, 2003) Cultural diversity has yet to transform the dominant narratives of most museums, galleries and the 'front stages' of city centres.

Many inner city areas, with a high concentration of decayed housing estates, sink schools, high levels of unemployment and poverty have acquired an ethnic stigma. Instead they should be seen as the product of market forces combined with separatist housing policies and the defensive desire for safety in numbers and cultural cohesion by ethnic groups threatened by racism. The combined effect has been to understand poverty as a product of ethnicity, as a personal attribute and failing of ethnic minority individuals. This is what it means to *ethnicise* poverty. Inevitably it attributes ethnic segregation to the unwillingness of minority ethnic groups to work or mix, rather than seeing it as a trap from which they cannot escape.

It is true that such ethnically segregated areas, housing and schools are found all over Western Europe, under different kinds of policy regimes, including: civic integration in France, the ethnic nationalist system of 'guestworkers' that has operated until recently in Germany or multicultural integration in the Netherlands, where there is more comprehensive welfare support and inclusive representation than in Britain. Yet multiculturalism has not counteracted, and may have served to consolidate these trends.

A number of key government reports, in response to the riots in Northern towns in 2001, have highlighted competition between white working class and poor immigrant areas in bidding for grant aid. (Ouseley Report, 2001, 11; Cantle Report, 2002, 25-26; Amin, 2002) In the people canvassed in both Ouseley's report on Bradford and the Cantle report on Oldham, Burnley and Bradford, government policies on housing, regeneration and education, were widely perceived as causing or exacerbating ethnic segregation. As a reaction to this segregation, different groups have begun to operate self-segregation, defensively retreating from contact, perceived on the one hand by some 'white' designated organisations, as motivated by separatism, traditionalism and religious fundamentalism, and on the other, by Asian communities, as motivated by racism and Islamophobia. (Ouseley Report, 2001, 10, 14, 16,18; Cantle Report, 2002, 7, 28-9; 59;) Both these reports use the concept of the 'white community' without addressing the contribution of 'white flight' to producing ethnic segregation through the effects on property prices and schools, shoring up what Amin defines as "white Englishness". (See Amin on this point, 2002; Kundnani, 2001, 106-7)

One effect of racially or ethnically imbued thinking on policy and communities is to ensure that 'others' are characterised from the outside as racially or ethnically fixed, with negative, unchanging traits and a singular community belonging. Treating other cultures as foreign or alien, holding them in a time warp of the past when they are cultural hybrids of here and now, assumes they have a static essence that does not adapt or absorb other influences. Racial and ethnic differences are taken as the defining differences in politics, often heightening differences of the most traditional kind, for example attributing a unified religious identity to Asians, or on the Continent to Maghrebins, as Muslim. The consequence of attributing a single identity and community belonging to ethnic minorities is to define a single racial or ethnic voice for each community. This is exacerbated by the claims of traditional leaders to speak with one voice, which has enabled them to exclude independent, dissident and pluralist voices of women (Yuval-Davis, 2000) and of young people of the second and third generation.

Where this has happened in Britain, in conjunction with segregated housing, separate neighbourhoods, separate council-funded youth and community centres, formerly broad inter-ethnic groupings have fragmented into different cultural or religious components. In Bradford, for example, Malik is right to point to how the Asian business community became institutionally divided along community lines with the creation in 1987 of the largely Hindu and Sikh Institute of Asian Businesses; in 1989 the Hindu Economic Development Forum; and in 1991, the Muslim-controlled Asian Business and Professional Club. Likewise with the Asian youth movement: "the beacon in the 1970s of a united struggle against racism, was split up, torn apart by such multicultural tensions". (Malik, 2002)

The counter-reaction among some young Muslim men, who have experienced social rejection at home – deprivation, discrimination, police harassment and racial violence, has been to identify themselves as Muslims with the most fundamentalist and repressive political expression of Islam internationally in Hizbollah, Hamas, Islamic Jihad and the Taliban. (e.g. for Oldham Ahmed, Bodi, Kazim and Shadjarreh, 2001) This phenomenon is not only found in declining Northern towns in Britain, but also in France. It highlights how ethnic characterisation that assumes an essential, traditional and singular view within a minority community and politically acts to entrench it, so fostering isolation and fundamentalism and undermining cultural renewal.

These shifts do not characterise the overall picture. Gert Baumann has shown the tendencies of the Asian youth movement to develop through its musical culture in an inter-ethnic direction in Southall. (Baumann, 1996, 1997) The inescapable realities of second and third generation are of more multiple belonging, criss-crossing identities, such as Euro-Islam, and trends of bilingualism, secularisation and intermarriage. This varies from place to place and across different ethnic groups in Europe. There are high rates of inter-marriage between African-Caribbeans and white British – 50% for men and over 40% for women. Turkish inter-marriage with white Dutch is approaching these levels, while, Asian rates are much lower. Young Turkish men in Germany are reverting to marriage with Turkish girls from rural parts of Turkey, not born or brought up in Germany. Other tendencies among British Asians are the growth of less traditional forms of family which may be linked to the strong educational and professional success of Indians and the greater independence this opens to those women. Examples of forced marriage and violence to wilful brides rightfully acquire notoriety, but to highlight them as typical as the media often does, or to exploit this image politically, as the Home Secretary, David Blunkett has done, gives a distorted picture overall of social change among British Asians.

Likewise, those who claimed that language – or rather a lack of English - was a precipitating factor in the riots, cannot have heard the thick northern accents with which Asian youths articulated their anger about their treatment at the hands of police, about racist assaults, lack of jobs and hope in their neighbourhoods. As Alibhai-Brown points out in *After Multiculturalism* bilingualism is an undervalued resource which banks and call centres have begun to recognise. (Alibhai-Brown, 2001) even though government has not. It is common to find second and third generation young people, Asian and Afro-Caribbean disavowing racial and ethnic characterisation of themselves, even in de-industrialised and depressed Northern towns. For example, Asif, a member of the recently formed Calderdale Youth Forum interviewed just after the riots, wanted to be defined simply as young, not Asian or black. (Harris and Bright, 2001) The desire to be defined as an individual and by achievement rather than colour or ethnicity is most commonly expressed by second and third generation artists, writers, musicians, directors across Western Europe. (Bloomfield, 2003, 114) They often plea not to be put back into an ethnic straitjacket.

These social and cultural changes have moved ahead of policy and communal outlooks. Where multiculturalism has encouraged identity politics and insufficiently addressed the social inequalities and injustices that generally underlie claims for recognition (Brown, 2001, 104-5) it has created conditions in which the minority's characteristics appear responsible for their differential treatment. When politicians attribute negative, singular characteristics to a minority group – such as their poor grasp of English – as the cause of their plight, they stigmatise the minority culture and can divert attention from both social and economic inequality and discrimination.

Some critical writers also tend to take groups as given and unproblematic 'communities of the oppressed', treating them as though they were homogenous, uniformly radical or 'insurgent' though Sandercock has moved away from this position in her latest work. (Sandercock, 1996; 2003) Without allowing for public criticism of inequalities and differences *within* minority communities, the internal dynamics of power within communities cannot be addressed, or just claims distinguished from politically contentious ones. All organised communities have leaders who seek to control their boundaries in order to retain their monopoly of representation and prevent criss-crossing, competing affiliations from becoming primary and supplanting them.

Public policy should not demonise 'the other', lumping them all together under one label, and failing to recognise the pluralism of belief within a group, the multiple attachments and belonging of individuals within any one group and the real inequalities that minority ethnic people in conflict face. Nor is it helpful to glorify oppressed communities, taking all the cultural and political manifestations of minorities as inherently positive, just and beyond debate.

False Alternatives to Multiculturalism

The critique we have made of multiculturalism is of its limitations and problems. However, there are those who want to deny the validity of multiculturalism *tout court.* (such as Kenan Malik and the Institute of Ideas) Yet reality is multicultural, and there is a need to address the shortcomings of policy outcomes and social fragmentation. Not all inequality is due to class. We have highlighted cases where conflicts are treated as though they are cultural, whereas in fact they are protests at disadvantage, discrimination and exclusion. Cultural denigration and misrepresentation are modern forms of racism that have detrimental, material effects on self-esteem, educational attainment, self organisation and public voice and so should be addressed in themselves.

On the other hand, critics previously favourable to multiculturalism have reacted to its perceived shortcomings by arguing for integration of ethnic minorities into a pre-constructed national identity or revamped 'Britishness'. In an earlier phase, Alibhai-Brown argued for "an organic community which is able to sustain diversity" (1999, 15) Trevor Phillips, the Chairman of the Commission for Racial Equality has recently denounced multiculturalism and now advocates integration into the pre-given nation state. (Phillips, 4.04.04; 26.04.04.)

Organic solidarity in a unified national community is not desirable and an unattainable goal in a complex, diverse society where people do not agree on cultural or spiritual values and lifestyles, whether immigrant or native born, whatever colour, national origin or belief we have. The common denominator between diverse people should be to stress the importance of democracy, which should provide the guarantee to have peaceful mechanisms for living with, and resolving where possible, political disagreements and living with differences that do not affect others' rights. And nobody denies that living with differences is difficult.

Communitarian arguments presume a national identity and common good, which is not open to debate or negotiation. The debate on national identity is hopelessly confused with competing and arbitrarily selected images which are often at variance. Is it the myth of Middle England? Is this represented by the Countryside Alliance or the 60 year old women who blocked the road to prevent the live export of animals? Is it the bulldog emblem coined by New Labour (Finlayson 2002) and its attempted refashioning of the UK in contemporary cultural light as Cool Britannia? All castings of national identity serve to define who really belongs and who is an outsider and thus exclude the socially 'undesirable'. This category is easily extended, as it has recently been in the *Prospect* magazine, to immigrants and asylum seekers, on the grounds that they are not like 'us', that they may not share 'our' civilised values. (Goodhart, 2003)

The more diffuse concept of community cohesion, employed in the Cantle Report (Cantle, 2000), also suffers from a lack of coherence.

Firstly it seeks to enhance cohesion around racially defined communities: the 'majority white community' and the 'minority, largely non-white community'. (Cantle, 19) To achieve this greater cohesion, it solicits more social control within them through establishing 'a set of clear values that can govern behaviour', ignoring the authoritarian and exclusionary consequences of this approach. At the same time it proposes greater involvement by the majority in getting to know other cultures and by the minority in national institutions and, greater participation, "especially of young people in shaping the Nation, agreeing common elements of nationhood". (Cantle, 2001 18-20). Yet while it advocates a more pluralist remaking of the nation, it sees globalisation as 'a threat to the identity of all races, cultures and nations', and thus prevents any new understanding of the history of migration and colonialism or appreciation of the plight of new migrants and asylum seekers.

The Parekh Report, on the other hand, which resulted from a non-governmental commission, set up by the Runnymede Trust, proposes a remaking of Britain as a nation of diverse citizens and communities, as 'a community of communities', that cannot be defined through Britishness. (Parekh, 2002, 36-39) This led to the report being disparaged by most of the press and disavowed by government, which meant its deep and far-reaching analysis of the crisis of national identity, the many different forms of racism and its many imaginative proposals were largely ignored. Like the government reports which succeeded it, it sought to combine social cohesion and communitarian ideals with a picture of porous community boundaries and multiple belonging, even of a legally enshrined right of individuals to opt out of a community – to which there is no legal, only ascribed or imaginary membership. Such an attempt to combine communitarianism which, by its nature, enforces communal norms, values or mores on individual 'members', with liberal values of liberty, confuses solidarity with reinforcing group boundaries and internal conformity.

This perspective prevents the Parekh Commission from seeing the potential for stripping Britishness of its racial and cultural connotations as white, Anglo-Saxon and Protestant. By stripping Britishness of particular racial and cultural features, it could become an all-encompassing, legal citizenship and 'thin' overarching civic identity. The kind of measures this requires would include disestablishing the Church of England, renegotiating the constitutional position of its constituent nations and regions on the basis of equality, and removing the racial bias from immigration and nationality law and administrative practice. It would entail implementing the range of measures the report recommends across all public and social institutions to undermine racial privilege and discrimination. This could also contribute to reviving the social basis of citizenship in welfare rights which emerged in Britain after the Second World War. Thus 'Britishness' could act as a universal civic and social container for multiple identities which have already gained currency, as the report recognises – such as British Asian, British Jew, black British, British Muslim and so on – and even multinational belonging – such as being Scottish and British - in an egalitarian multinational state.

Such a reformed, legal basis of citizenship would be underpinned by democratic values, political organisation and social rights, not based on racially or ethnically defined communities, but on free political association and collective self-organisation in local and national public spheres and on social need, that combines liberal rights of the individual with active republican citizenship.

Cultural Diversity and Civic Values

It is true cultural diversity requires certain shared values for us to live together. These overarching values would be civic in character though, not based on selective cultural requirements or particularities of belief and practice. From civic values we derive general rules which are shared in the political community, or public sphere, such as reciprocal respect as democratic equals, agreed procedures for organising and expressing disagreement, mechanisms of debate and for reaching agreement, access to the media and means of information and persuasion. Cultural differences among citizens should not be held as a bar to political participation on an equal footing. The representation of immigrants as politically suspect or 'un-British' – if they cheer a West Indian cricket team, or speak a communal language in the home other than English, confuses cultural difference with citizenship in a political community. Likewise, requiring immigrants who are applying for citizenship to swear an oath of allegiance to the Queen and her successors, when no British-born subject has to, implies potential disloyalty and is thus discriminatory. But groups organised around their cultural differences who make claims on the political system for resources, recognition or against discrimination, as other interest groups do, are equally entitled to press their case and try and win wider public support, change public perception, policy and practice of institutions.

The full and active participation of all groups in the political process, at many different levels and in different forms is a prerequisite for achieving a thriving, inclusive, intercultural democracy. It inevitably entails ongoing dialogue, in which groups develop greater self-awareness and also criss-crossing alliances, and with them a capacity for strategic thinking and framing of alternative policies. This creates a more receptive framework for addressing claims of ethnic injustice and discrimination where people have a real chance of being heard and winning public support.

Negotiating differences helps shape culturally sensitive services and planning and in developing an intercultural public culture, where the diverse public enlarges its knowledge and empathy of others and becomes aware of their needs and the justice or otherwise of their claims. However, a process of dialogue does not reach an endpoint. This may result in giving priority to the needs of the most disadvantaged and discriminated against, but more often than not lead to stalemates, compromises or only partial shifts and the continuation of struggles and unresolved conflicts. This is a vision of universalism which is *arrived at* through an ongoing process, not readymade. It does not extinguish the plurality of opinions and beliefs, but seeks to engage them creatively to solve problems.

Such a view of deliberative democracy has republican dimensions of actively fostering collective self-organisation, voice and representation as an adjunct to the formal party political system. It is distinguished from an uncritical consensual ideal of living together in difference. The terms of engagement require mutual respect as a starting point and giving up monopolistic claims to dominance or superiority. Santos De Sousa has suggested the terms on which intercultural dialogue between widely differing world outlooks and cultures can most fruitfully proceed. This progresses by exploring key concepts and themes (*topoi*) which are held in common, highlighting the strengths and weaknesses of their interpretation as seen from the point of view of the other, and synthesising those elements which together produce the most universal, inclusive outcome. (See Santos De Sousa, 1995; 1999)

This approach may presume too much difference or that differences derive from 'incommensurate' cultures while most urban conflicts in contemporary post-industrial societies are, as Iris Marion Brown points out, responses to structural inequalities rather than fundamental cultural differences. (Brown, 2002, 105) Santos De Sousa (1995; 1999) also suggests that those strands and representatives that are most inclusive and universal within any one cultural tradition should be chosen rather than the most particularist elements, which are most at odds with the other. However, in conflict situations it is important to engage with the organisations and voices of people involved. A city council does not have the luxury of selecting the leaders and representatives of oppositional groups, especially young people. The city has to try and engage them in dialogue from which they have previously been excluded, that has often been a precipitating cause of riots in Britain and France.

Brown's work (2002) is important for defining some of the optimum conditions for intercultural dialogue. Intercultural dialogue will erode the idea of a 'majority white community' and dominant culture and replace it with a politically constituted democratic majority on the one hand, and an intercultural public sphere and public services on the other.

Why Interculturalism?

Shared Existence and Solidarity
What is the imperative for interculturalism, rather than multiculturalism? How can and should we live with difference? As argued, we need to ground cultural diversity in both individual autonomy, collective self-organisation and presence within the local public sphere. Yet to ensure the collective organisation, public presence and voice of ethnic minorities it is not sufficient to create wider inter-ethnic alliances, alternative policies, culturally sensitive services and a diverse, inclusive public realm. Solidarity can only be built on shared existence. Solidarity implies we are all part of one human family whatever our national, racial, religious, economic or ideological differences. Only when people meet and mix in everyday life can they get to know and understand the needs and feelings of others and develop those 'moral sympathies for the other' on which a shared civil life can grow. So the city has to promote interaction between different cultural groups to cultivate mutual respect and overcome the insensitivity and stereotyping that is a product of ignorance, rather than racist ideology or gut hatred.

Urban policy should thus be geared to peaceful civic co-existence, social and cultural mixing and getting to know the other and thus actively counter tendencies to ethnic segregation. It is not viable for a city to foster or permit territorial segregation on the grounds of the voluntary desire of an ethnic group to live together to support the continuity of their identity – language, religion or history that Iris Marion Young considers legitimate. (Young, 2000, 210-235) The desire for people to retain a group by clustering together *per se* does not create ethnic segregation of the kind that has emerged in West European cities which Brown recognises exists.

Ethnic segregation often emerges from a failure of planning which leads to a very high or exclusive territorial concentration of an ethnic minority in one area. The boundaries of the group thus coincide almost exclusively with the spatial boundaries of the local neighbourhood: housing estate, workplace, school catchment area, shops and social facilities so there is virtually no social overlap with any other group. This frequently means that ethnic minority families are dumped in the poorest areas, with the least endowed and maintained schools, the most degraded environment and housing. Not only does this structure inequalities into the spatial fabric of the city it also prevents the sharing of social space and experience with others which create the common ground for empathy and solidarity.

Ethnic minorities only in exceptional circumstances choose exclusive spatial seclusion and social isolation. Usually this derives from mechanisms of exclusion by the state and market, not the voluntary desire for group affiliation and cultural protection. It tends to happen through segregationist housing allocation and management policies in public housing, veiled selective mechanisms in state education by religion and background, 'white flight' and the attendant effects on house prices and the mix in schools.

A cosmopolitan city has to address the obstacles to intercultural mixing by countering tendencies to spatial and social segregation, separatist tendencies expressed in religious-based schools and a retreat into traditionalism. Such a strategy calls for initiatives to 'de-ethnicise' poverty, for example by preventing competition for funding in inner city areas between ethnic minorities and white working-class areas, by involving competing districts in deciding what is just and which bids should be prioritised. This entails a shift to allocation on the basis of needs, not ethnicity. The city has to act to remove the ethnic stigma that blights particular inner city areas and spaces –

through co-ordinated regeneration, city marketing, communications and community safety initiatives of which some imaginative examples already exist. (see Chapter 4) To counter ethnic segregation in urban space, regeneration and local economic development strategies have to be designed to keep areas mixed or enhance their mix against the strong market pressures to force out low income households and reduce the cultural mix, 'whitewashing' inner city areas.

Equally ethnic segregation in schooling and cultural institutions, while not purely spatial in character, calls for imaginative policy intervention to counteract unintended consequences and cumulative effects of individuals' movements by positively redirecting them. For example, art-led strategies can actively attract back middle class, white pupils whom schools have lost, attaining a greater cultural mix. Likewise, city centre cultural institutions such as theatres, concert halls and galleries, which have become taboo places for ethnic minorities, can attract a diverse public if they rethink the practice of the institution in an intercultural light, addressing the ambience of the place, the mix of personnel at all levels, including management, the mix of the programme, culturally sensitive marketing and pricing.

An intercultural public sphere is predicated on creating a single diverse public not multiple publics which are organisationally and socially separate. The idea of separate publics reinforces ethnic segregation of the public sphere rather than overcoming it. When Amin refers to micro publics – he is referring to micro public spaces which make possible cultural mixing. Ethnic segregation can only be overcome within a uniform public sphere which confers equal rights of access and participation and obligations of citizenship, but at the same time reflects the pluralistic character of its citizens and their cultural make-up. There is no room for no-go areas or ghettoes of confinement or polycentric cities without a shared centre. (Beauregard and Body-Gendrot, 1999, 5-6) The voluntary fellowships of faith, cultural and intellectual exchange, political action, sport are not carried out primarily on an ethnic basis, but on the basis of common interests, beliefs or values, that require shared physical and social spaces, centres and meeting places.

If community is reconceived not as singular, bounded and ascribed but as multiple, criss-crossing attachments, identities and forms of belonging, then it becomes clear that 'minorities' overlap with and are constitutive of the 'majority' in many contexts. This would address the complaints of minorities of their lack of acceptance by the majority population and their desire for further integration. (See for example, Kelso and Vasagar J. *The Guardian* 17.06.02) As all people occupy overlapping 'subject positions', (Hall 1992, 1996) none of us has a single community or place of belonging, as it is layered by movement to different cities, regions or countries, criss-crossed by other group affiliations around occupation, language, culture, faith, political belief. We are also not tied exclusively to one history or territory (Alibhai-Brown, 2000, 271) whether migrant country of origin or constituent nation of Britain as now we are also part of the wider European Union - an additional political community which adds another layer to our individual identities.

Baumann's findings from his research among Southall young Asians shows both a dominant discourse in use which assigns a quasi racial character to local communities as Asians, Caribbeans and whites and a further subdivision of Asians into Sikh, Hindu and Muslim, and what he terms 'demotic discourse' - a popular counter language and frame of reference. This challenged the assignment of a given culture to a singular community. He found Hindu Southallians who interpreted their faith as including other communities including lower caste Sikhs; he spoke to Pan-Africanist Afro Caribbeans who wanted to make a culture for themselves that they had historically been denied; an Asian youth movement which cut across traditional religious, regional, class and caste divides through Bhangra music. "The discovery of an 'Asian' culture among the young presents an apt example of the processes by which 'culture' and 'community' become objects of debate and terms of cross-'community' exploration". (Baumann, 1996, 1997, 219)

Despite the press equations of headscarves and *hijab* with self-evident orthodoxy and anti-Western sentiment, Muslim girls present an equally complex picture of their identity. In France, they have used the headscarf to negotiate social space to mix with other French students, while retaining their personal and religious identity within the authority relations of school and family. They have claimed their rights to education – as citizens of the republic – and to personal expression of their faith. (See, Gaspard and Khosrow-Khavar 1995; Yuval Davis, 2000)

What are the implications for cities of multiple identities and communities not being fixed? How can cities foster cross-over and inter-ethnic affinities and build on the already existing commonalities which are the basis of intercultural solidarity? For a start, they need to stop addressing ethnic minority communities in exclusive terms, no longer characterising them in a singular and traditional fashion as though they were unchanging and adjust their political appeals, funding mechanisms and programmes accordingly. Not only does multiple identification have implications for how you address people, but for how you categorise them, collect statistical data and carry out cultural and ethnic monitoring. In the 2001 census, a new category of mixed ethnicity showed it was the largest single ethnic group at 15%. How can the value of this growing group of people with mixed ethnicities be harnessed to creative advantage for the city?

The Parekh report foresaw a special role for people of mixed ethnicity as intercultural mediators. Such a role is already being developed in the psychotherapeutic and social sphere and in youth and community work, as for example, practised in intercultural centres in Turin and Brussels. (on the mediation work of the Intercultural Centre in Turin, see Ferrero ed. 2003; for Brussels see, for example, youth workshop with a Dito Dito theatre company in Houari, Hadj and Thomas, September 2000) The potential for intercultural mediators goes much wider - in neighbourhoods as housing and estate managers, in youth and community work doing projects with disaffected teenagers and gangs, in social and probation work, in adoption, in the health service, in clinics, in school as educational psychologists, in planning, consultation and civil disputes, facilitating exchange and the resolution of conflicts

Sandercock also outlines a new role for planners in addressing the host population's fear of the unknown and of change, confronting and dealing with feelings of hatred and nostalgia for a disappearing way of life that require special skills of listening, facilitating dialogue, drawing out differences through diverse forms of expression and working them through. (Sandercock, 2003, 137-8; 162-66) Once again people from mixed backgrounds, well versed in cultural adaptation and negotiation, would be adept as advisors and trainers in intercultural literacy throughout the professions and public institutions.

Cities can create new mechanisms of participation and engagement, what are called *political opportunity structures*, that give incentives to unrepresented or marginalised people to organise a collective presence and voice. As argued, a redistribution of political-organisational resources and capacities runs counterpart to measures of economic and social equality. City authorities can foster an equal basis of engagement among ethnic minorities, for example, by setting up inter-ethnic and inter-faith forums to establish a unified voice on shared concerns, to shape and culturally attune services in planning, health and welfare, and to allow dialogue and airing of differences that can reduce or resolve disputes.

Cultural Renewal and Innovation

Solidarity is the commonly held ground for interculturalism, but we want to put forward other, less commonly heard grounds. We have resisted multicultural and communitarian concepts of integration into a pre-existing culture and community, challenging ideas of fixed ethnic minorities and an ethnic majority, in favour of cultural renewal. This alternative seeks to challenge the dominance of the given culture, with its unspoken assumptions of superiority, and the marginal status of minority ethnic and sub-cultures as a model of their relationship which leads to closure in both. It cuts the dominant culture off from critical perspectives and alternative traditions, ideas and artistic forms and minority cultures from influence on the mainstream. By bringing them in from the margin, they can bear on and reshape the dominant culture, contributing to remaking a shared public culture in an intercultural way.

To move forward with interculturalism the state and cities should foster cultural renewal. On the one hand, an inclusive democratic society cannot justify excluding or marginalising ethnic minority citizens, or excluding their histories, stories and expressive forms from the mainstream culture. In a pluralist, post-colonial society, the dominant national narrative of unbroken continuity of British history, the island race, the unbroken military prowess and colonial superiority, constitutional moderation, pragmatism and fair play and so on (see the Parekh Report, 2002, 14-26 for the best account of rethinking national identity) cannot remain intact. An intercultural approach would involve the state and cities equally connecting minority cultures to the rest of society to prevent their isolation and marginalisation. Cities can aid cultural adaptation, helping second and third generation young people to develop their own political and artistic expression, easing problems of modernisation of religious institutions adjusting to a different cultural setting, while also supporting dynamic and vital elements of cultures through funding meeting places, cultural centres, and joint production projects.

New forms, products, processes and services are established through cross-fertilisation, not purification. Taking culture and art as an example, the new British Asian art forms offer a prolific instance in terms of musical review, stand-up comedy, Bollywood stage production and film, crossover video and live theatre with successful transfers to the West End and abroad. In dance Shobana Jeyasingh has fused classical Indian dance with European ballet, becoming a leader in the European avant garde. Keith Khan, the artistic director of Moti Roti, drew on his Indian Caribbean background in a fusion of Carnival, street theatre, Indian classical traditions and forms in his orchestration of the Queen's Jubilee in 2002. (Terracciano, 2002)

This same explosive mix can be found in commercial textile and fashion, industries, design, cuisine and music. Although these are largely cultural industries, this innovative drive cannot be accounted for simply as the trading and marketing of exotic difference in a globalised consumer market, as some critics have argued. (Friedman, 1990; 199; Cohen, 2000) They are based on production of goods and services, not just consumption. International research points to high levels of migrant motivation and social capital, embodied in family and communal networks, which are mobilised as alternative sources of credit, trade links and social support in creating small businesses. (Portes, 1995; 1997; Kontos, 2000) This points to a capacity to improvise and find alternatives when access to financial capital, education or further training are blocked. It is important to tap into and harness this drive to the benefit of the city, exploring for example, the potential of poor people's credit associations and of trade and touring networks.

Meeting and mixing and working together collaboratively across cultural traditions and disciplinary divides, shakes up given ways of doing and seeing things which has proved highly productive. So fostering openness to diverse and unfamiliar cultural influences promises significant gains in economic, as well as cultural, social and civic innovation. However, 'contamination' from other cultural traditions, can produce defensive and hostile responses to change which cities have to understand and counter – in novel ways such as those suggested by intercultural mediation and planning. This overall process promotes the broad economic gains through new businesses, services, products and through new organisational and financial forms.

Innovation is a powerful incentive for cities to become intercultural if they want to maximise the creative energy and productive outputs of cultural diversity. Yet this case is rarely made because the struggle for cultural recognition of ethnic minorities, many of whom feel oppressed, has taken precedence over the need for cultural renewal. Interculturalism requires policies that foster and reward innovation economically, culturally, organisationally, that embed intercultural enterprises and practices, and that foster intercultural collaborations. Such policies include investment in intercultural experiments – pilot schemes in planning and landscaping, in finance, insurance and banking services for poor people and excluded groups such as Muslims; commissioning work or sponsoring competitions that have a brief to combine classical and new, indigenous and foreign forms in architecture, urban and housing design, public art, sculpture, monuments. Such commissions should also include artistic and craft traditions from other cultures that would otherwise die out without a contemporary infusion. These kind of exemplary schemes should be matched by much wider and open tendering to diversify contractor firms.

Cities can facilitate the adaptation of religious institutions to the vernacular even where the state has not authorised training of imams, by fostering open dialogue in inter-faith and wider forums on controversial issues which touch Muslim communities, for example, such as schooling, Islamophobia, Kashmir. Thus they can encourage the development of a public Muslim presence in civic organisation and dialogue which recognises the plurality of Muslim schools of thought and sects, supporting the emergence of a hybrid EuroIslam.

Innovation should involve the teaching and certification of minority languages in school, according them equal intellectual status with European languages and the promotion of professional career paths with minority languages as social workers and health workers, community interpreters and cultural diversity and race awareness trainers that the Parekh Report called for, (Parekh, 2002, 290) or as intercultural literacy trainers as we have redefined them. Intercultural literacy is increasingly required in all kinds of occupation and profession, including for council officers and public administrators.

The Pluralist Reshaping of the Public Sphere
If citizenship is stripped of any particular culture and cultural dominance is to be dismantled, then public culture can be remade

collaboratively and interculturally. To undermine the dominant cultural monopoly, we have to recognise the composite nature of the city and embody it in civic institutions, symbols and celebrations through which citizens recognise they belong.

A new kind of intercultural, migrant or urban theatre, for instance, has emerged from the conventional confines of a sacred building onto the street. It is capable of symbolically re-enacting civic conflicts and co-existence that has been used to inaugurate intercultural spaces in the city or to represent the diverse cultural life of a great public institution such as a hospital back to its staff. (See Part III and Bloomfield, 2003)

The public sphere needs to become pluralist so it can reflect the diversity of its citizens. This touches on an intercultural re-reading of history and memory despite the claim (Paquot in Bearegard and Body-Gendrot, 1999. 84) that the modern city is the factory of novelty. This view cannot be sustained if you consider the institutions which shape popular representations of the past and national narratives: museums, public art, symbolic statues as well as the guided tours, tourist promotion, history texts and programmes.

Reshaping institutions and urban policies to include the viewpoint and experience of the other, revises the overall perspective and produces new professional needs for cultural animateurs and programmers who are interculturally trained. The Porto Franco project in Tuscany, for instasnce, offers an ambitious strategy of intercultural reinterpretation of the region's history and intervention to change public consciousness and mentality.

The establishment of intercultural institutions such as the Rich Mix Centre in London and to a lesser extent, the Werkstatt der Kulturen in Berlin, are in the forefront of re-evaluating national and migrant cultures and in showcasing the productivity of migration and cultural mixing. These kinds of initiatives need to spread from a rare exception to the rule, reaching the symbolic front stages of the city, its key symbols and high cultural institutions. Otherwise they run the risk of being marginalised again, acting as a token concession to ethnic minorities, rather than shaking up and transforming the mainstream.

If the public sphere is to become diverse rather than ethnic minority integration into a pre-existing whole, this will entail more public debate, frictions, confrontations and mediations, for "In the ideal democratic city, the walls have fallen. Across the divides of difference, people connect; they agree to differ". (Beauregard R. and Body Gendrot S., 1999, 14) We have proposed what is termed procedural democracy and republican citizenship, with a thin overarching civic culture removing cultural requisites for citizenship. Numerous problems have been raised in achieving this: unequal access to the media and political system, unequal organisational resources of the poor and marginal, misrepresentation and distortion of speech by those more powerful and in the know about public exposition and other limits on deliberative democracy such as rhetorical devices for presenting one's own view as representative of the 'nation' or of right-minded people, which undermines the legitimacy of dissent. (Fainstein in Beauregard and Body-Gendrot, 1999, 257; Brown 36-51) These obviously adversely affect the negotiated outcomes of pluralist debate but republican citizenship is not just about polite speech and appeals to officials, but concerns more robust collective self-organisation, and mobilisation around conflicts and the articulation of an alternative vision and policies, making political alliances and developing a capacity for strategic intervention and change.

Intercultural ethics are needed to avoid the worst tendency of identity politics – a concern only for one's own group that leads to fragmentation. What should these ethics consist of? What attributes are appropriate to the public domain in an intercultural context? Some starting points concern defending the distinction between public and private in culture, so as individuals you are not deprived of your personal identity and you do not stop being a distinctive individual with a particular culture in public. However, your behaviour should and generally does change. Normally you do not disclose your full private person to the whole world. You have to negotiate with strangers about whom you may know nothing. It is a problem when people carry over or prioritise their private interactions in public – such as talking loudly on their mobile phones for all to hear or knocking into people who are actually present because they are so taken up with their private conversation. These banal examples show the importance of mutual and general respect for those who are strangers to you and paradoxically the importance of prioritising those physically present, though unknown, over those familiar to you who are absent. Public intercultural ethics in essence focus on considering the needs of strangers. This may be a source of difficulty because it makes you aware of your necessary ignorance of them.

Respect has different dimensions to it – some of which have been touched on already - listening to other people's stories and issues without stereotyping a group by the actions of an individual as the press so frequently does. Being open to learning about others' cultural beliefs and practices and, most of all their meanings is an intercultural expression of curiosity. Including diverse celebrations and commemoration of tragedy into civic remembrance and festivals – for example through specially designated days in honour of different peoples symbolically sharing their history, suffering or achievement and making it your own.

Other kinds of respect include secular respect for sacred places, temples or burial grounds of people of other beliefs and histories and respect for places that commemorate their genocide and suffering. Likewise there is a need for intercultural respect for people of other faiths and their cultural heritage, temples or burial grounds even where they were founded on Christian or Muslim domination. Such ethics need to be taught not just by schools taking children on visits but by the churches and mosques. All the religious bodies need to be involved with secular educational organisations in public discussion on intercultural ethics.

Finally the precondition for deliberative democracy and republican citizenship lies in respect for your adversary without which you cannot become negotiating partners. The ethical imperative to live together should propel adversaries to build on what they have in common, rather than what divides them, seek the most universalistic solutions, foregrounding what is most just for all, not just for yourself or your own group.

PART TWO

Different Approaches to Cultural Diversity

Different countries have defined multiculturalism in different ways: as separate ethnic communities and cultures, the national cultures of origin of foreigners, the private culture of citizens who share a common public culture, cultural pluralism based on strands of different cultures that intertwine and create something new. These different definitions derive from different national self-understandings of power, place in the world, culture and of the position of others, which framed thinking and policy-making in the era of nation state building and colonialism. In the post-war era of decolonisation and post-colonial migration, the legacy of these conceptions has shaped the way states came to terms with the realities of economic reconstruction, consumer capitalism based on a mass migrant working class and a new international order.

Five distinctive policy approaches to immigration, integration and citizenship are defined with reference to particular countries with which each approach is closely associated:

- corporate multiculturalism in Britain and the Netherlands;
- civic integration in France;
- the 'melting pot' approach and drift to ethnic essentialism in the US;
- ethnic nationalism and the *Gastarbeiter* system in Germany;
- the Southern European laissez-faire unregulated regime in countries of former emigration, and its shift to a restrictive regime as countries of new immigration.

We also consider 'transculturalism', a sixth approach to cultural diversity which derived from international organisations such as UNESCO and has influenced some cities.

Corporate Multiculturalism

This approach is based on the recognition of diverse ethnic communities and their representation as groups in political bargaining and resourcing at local level, as a supplement rather than alternative to the democratic political system. Although it takes a more institutionalised form in the Netherlands with, for example, proportional representation of minorities on consultative committees, nevertheless both Britain and the Netherlands treat ethnic minorities as part of distinctive communities and cultures. Corporate multiculturalism tries to protect community boundaries and traditional authority and so necessarily limits intergenerational renewal and intercultural communication. As a policy approach, it has largely failed to build on the plurality of affiliations and the new kinds of identity that have emerged with subsequent generations born here. Such an approach would facilitate interaction between different communities across cultural boundaries and cultural renewal.

Britain

British colonialism was distinguished from the French by its laissez faire approach to the colonised, seeking to control them through public order and institutions, rather than by imposing its own culture very directly. Consequently, the British approach was determined more by "managing public order and relations between majority and minority populations... allowing ethnic cultures and practices to mediate the process". (Favell, 1998, 4)

Labour migration from the West Indies after the war and during the 1950s, and from India and Pakistan mainly in the 1960s was solicited by the state to fill jobs in the health and transport services, although recruitment was left largely to the market. (Peach, CRER,1991) From the late 40s throughout 1950s immigration went on under the 1948 Nationality Act, which treated post-colonial Commonwealth subjects as British citizens. This open door policy lasted until 1962. From the 1962 Commonwealth Immigrants Act immigration was restricted by job vouchers to filling shortages in the economy and then racially through 'patrial status' confining immigration to those who had a parent or grandparent born in the U.K. From 1971 black immigration was thus confined to family reunion. (Spencer, 1997, 143-44) The stridently nationalist Thatcher Nationality Act 1981, stopped even black family reunion and withdrew the centuries old entitlement of children born in Britain of non-British parents to *ius solis* - automatic citizenship at birth on the territory.

However, despite the restrictions, black and Asian migration, based mainly on family reunion continued up to the 1980s at between 30-50,000 a year. In 1972 a wave of Ugandan Asians were allowed in as refugees, swelling the numbers in that year to 60,000. (Spencer, 1, 133) They formed a small business class that rapidly revitalised Britain's ailing corner shops and post offices. Chinese and Bangladeshis came to Britain during the 1980s – the Chinese were already well established in catering and began to advance professionally, while the Bangladeshis, from poor rural backgrounds, became heavily concentrated in inner city pockets of textile manufacture, especially in Tower Hamlets in east London. During the 1980s and 1990s, many black Africans came as refugees from such places as Nigeria, Liberia and Zaire. Ethnic minorities as a whole now constitute 7.9% of the overall population, i.e. 4.6 million out of a population of 58 million, most of them citizens, highly concentrated in London where 45% of all ethnic minorities live, and in a few other big cities in the Midlands and North. (2001 Census)

A dualist approach was adopted of racially restricted immigration combined with piecemeal integration within a legal framework that formed the consensus between left and right. Race relations legislation, outlawing discrimination in jobs and housing was enacted by a Labour Government: the 1968 Race Relations Act also banned incitement to racial hatred and the 1976 Act extended the ban from direct to indirect discrimination and required schools to acknowledge religious and cultural identities. A Commission for Racial Equality was set up to monitor racial discrimination and bring test cases to court.. Although the legal framework sought to protect individuals, politically government sought mediation through community leaders. Ethnic mobilisation of Asians, particularly by the Labour Party, took place at local level, to win marginal inner city constituencies.

However, the pragmatic bent of British policy, in contrast to the Dutch meant that social integration was largely left to the market and civil society, rather than active government intervention. As a result of delayed and poor access to council housing many West Indians and Asians bought up cheap inner city houses. (Karn, Kemeny, Williams, 1985, 52: 2) The government's shift away from comprehensive redevelopment under which the white working class had been rehoused in outlying high rise estates, to cheaper urban renewal programmes which shored up the old housing stock in the inner cities, reinforced ethnic segregation and 'the privatisation of squalor'. (Karn, Kemeny, Williams, 1985, 105; Smith, 1987, 30)

Social conflict broke through the consensus and provoked a patttern – of disturbances, followed by judicial inquiry and reactive political response. Young black people mobilised in inner city riots against police violence and social abandonment in 1981 and in 1985. (recalled in the Steel Pulse album *Handsworth Revolution*) The Scarman report in the wake of the first riots recommended community friendly policing and substantial funding to address inner city deprivation. The reports triggered retroactive government intervention with special urban programmes. However, nationally, a cultural rather than welfare approach gained the upper hand, with the introduction of teaching diverse faiths and cultures but not institutional change or social measures to address racism and inequality. (Favell, 1998, 131) This remains a key contrast with the Netherlands where multicultural education has been combined with an ongoing commitment to high level welfare.

In the 1990s, mobilisation was led by the families of victims of racially motivated murder who challenged the police, the judicial system, and race relations as a whole. The Macpherson Inquiry, brought about by the campaign for justice by the parents of Stephen Lawrence, an 18 year old victim of racial murder, condemned the police for institutional racism and made recommendations that are now becoming law on rooting out discriminatory practices in all public institutions. Some cities at the sharp end, like Birmingham, have begun to address ingrained ethnic inequality, through a targeted, non-ethnic, needs-based approach and new kinds of participation through inter-ethnic and inter-faith council. The second generation, especially women and young people have also begun to organise independently of their elders for example, the Southall Black Sisters and Bengali Youth Forum in Spitalfields, East London, diversifying the voice and representation in these communities. Thus multiculturalism is evolving at local level against separatist trends, in a more pluralist and intercultural direction.

However at national level, the government remains committed to a communitarian approach. Despite the findings of the Cantle Report, on the cause of riots in the North of England in 2001, of the lack of social and cultural contact between different communities, the government has recently allowed separate Muslim schools, on a par with other state funded denominational schools, that are likely to increase ethnic segregation. It has also attributed blame for the riots to the cultural failure of Asians to speak English at home, although the rioters had immaculate northern accents, rather than addressing social causes.

The British approach has been re-examined in the light of the Macpherson Report, the Cantle Report following the riots in the North in 2001, and Birmingham's own Stephen Lawrence Commission of Inquiry. The ensuing debate has been more open to considering alternative policy frameworks for cultural diversity, although none has been explicitly intercultural. A perceptible shifted has taken place over the last few years from a corporate form of multiculturalism to cultural diversity at city level. This change has not been expressed in government, but has been strongly promoted in the cultural sector by the Arts Council.

The Netherlands
In the post-war period, the prevalent view until the late 1970s was that the Netherlands was overpopulated and a country of emigration not immigration. The foreign resident population stood at a mere 120,000 out of a population of 15 million. (Lucassen and Penninx, 1994, 11) It changed view under the confluence of two different streams of immigration.

The first wave in the 1960s was formed by temporary labour recruitment from Turkey and Morocco of guestworkers without settlement rights or citizenship. But despite the denial of being a country of immigration, no restriction was imposed on family reunion as it was elsewhere, so by the late 1970s, families began to settle. (Lucassen and Penninx, 1998, 149) The legacy was a population of 280,000 Turks and 233,000 Moroccans in 1997. (Vermeulen and Penninx, 1998, 9) In the 1970s, the second stream of immigration came from the post-colonial influx from the Dutch East Indies – mainly Java. The Indonesians became Dutch citizens, but the state sought to assimilate them rather than acknowledge their culture. In 1975 with the onset of Surinamese independence, there was a further migration from Surinam and the Dutch Antilles to acquire Dutch citizenship before restrictions were imposed.

However, with the general stop on labour migration after 1973-4, clandestine migration of *sans papiers,* undocumented workers, increased to the cities. The current wave of newcomers are asylum seekers particularly from Iran, Iraq, Algeria and Morocco. Thus, Dutch multiculturalism, unlike British, has encompassed a range of minorities who came with different statuses from post-colonial and *Gastarbeiter* migration regimes. Although long settled, the minorities combined amount to only 5.7% of the Dutch population. (Lecassen and Penninx, 1998, 172)

Up till the late 1970s, policies were based on the myth of the Neatherlands as an immigrant nation, but by the early 1980's a series of reports began to shift policy from the implausible position to one of policy recognition of immigrant minorities. The new minorities policy aimed to create a multicultural society in which distinctiveness was valued, and group associations would play the key part in maintaining immigrant culture and identity. This approach was mediated by welfare measures to counter social disadvantage and discrimination in line with equal opportunities. Like the British, state action was directed at removing obstacles to voluntary initiative and community development, and eliminating discriminatory practices. But the Dutch state was more proactive and institutionalised in its approach establishing national and local consultative councils of each minority, composed of delegates from the major immigrant associations, promoting 'proportional distribution' and even-handed treatment. (Entzinger, 1994, 27)

Unlike in Britain, the gap in treatment of citizens and aliens was gradually bridged since the early 1980s. Aliens' legal position has been secured so they can obtain permanent residence after five years, those who enter for purposes of family reunion gain permanency after three years. The citizenship law of 1985 gave third generation children of parents born in the Netherlands automatic nationality –ius soli and second generation children of resident aliens brought up in the Netherlands the right to opt for Dutch nationality at 18-25 years of age. It also eased naturalisation and dual citizenship, thus producing a high 5% naturalisation. Consequently, over half the Turkish community has a Dutch passport. Foreigners also have the right to stand and vote in local elections and since 1986 several have been elected onto councils in the bigger cities. A comprehensive bill for Equal Treatment of Immigrants was passed in 1994 which outlaws unequal treatment on the basis of nationality, ethnicity, religion, sex, age and other grounds.

In housing special new build rented accommodation was allocated to citizens from former colonies, but not *Gastarbeiter.* From the 1980s the government sought to outlaw discrimination in the private rented sector but minorities remain at a disadvantage there, exacerbated by the government withdrawal from public provision of housing in the 1990s. Within the framework of corporate bargaining between employers and unions, still in tact in the Netherlands in 1990 unlike the UK, strong measures were taken to counter the high unemployment among minorities.

In education the Dutch state interpreted equal opportunity in terms of special support for language learning with the close involvement of parents, and accorded equal status to minority cultures in the curriculum, providing for the teaching of minority language and culture. 'Intercultural education' was also instituted to incorporate immigrant culture and history into the general curriculum. The prior framework of Dutch 'pillarisation' which had divided the spoils of power between the different social groups - Protestant, Catholic and Liberal secular, provided a ready-made framework of regulation for Muslims and Hindus to set up their own schools, as began to happen after 1988. This runs counter to the more individualised and secularised society which had led to the erosion of pillarised confessional politics in the 1970s and remains a source of tension. However, the Diyanet, the main organisation of Turkish mosques is committed to a Europeanised form of Islam, aiming at Dutch trained imams to attract the 2nd generation of Dutch-speaking Turks back to the mosque. (van Amersfoort H. and Doomernik J., 1997)

The Dutch approach remains highly institutionalised and prescriptive, in terms of quotas and formal representation of ethnic minorities in different institutions, for example the media. However, it has become increasingly flexible and open to intercultural experiments especially in education. Whilst the Dutch understanding of multiculturalism has been more underpinned than the British by an understanding of social deprivation based on class not cultural difference, the weaknesses in Dutch multiculturalism are most evident there. Unemployment rates for Turks and Moroccans stood at 21% and 36% in the early 1990s, and these are also the groups excluded from social housing. Moreover, they are portrayed as welfare dependent and unwilling to adapt, particularly by improving their Dutch. This testifies not so much to the failure of corporate multiculturalism, as to that of the *Gastarbeiter* system which stigmatised and excluded them for so long.

Civic Cultural Integration: the French approach

France is characterised by a strong tradition of civic republicanism, based on a concept of the nation as a political community of equals, a secular state with universal rights, which find their origin in the Revolution of 1789. It is into this political community that immigrants from the colonies have been integrated as citizens. The French universalist ideal of integration aimed to transform immigrants into '*citoyens*' since the cultural requisites of citizenship are acquired through socialisation, rather than inherited, hence the great emphasis on language and education. (Favell, 1998) Civic equality has been publicly embodied in high quality services and public spaces, but until recently, this has happened within an assumption of the cultural uniformity of what it means to be French – symbolised by the French language as the embodiment of civilisation, guarded against American contamination, the grandeur of State culture, the regional cheeses and wines of *la France profonde*. However, this has been misrepresented as an 'assimilationist' model (e.g. Entzinger, 1994, 20), whereas it has guaranteed private association and cultural practice, and enabled second generation immigrants to contest what it means to be French and organise to push 'French' culture in a pluralistic direction.

In immigration terms, *ius sanguinis*, citizenship by descent, is supplemented by *ius soli*, citizenship acquired by birth in the territory. Sizeable labour migration since the 19[th]C took place without state concern –enabling easy naturalisation as figures on French nationals show: between a sixth and a quarter of them have at least one foreign-born grandparent. In 1999 out of population of 60 million, there were 3.5 million foreigners and about 10 million 'of foreign origin' (i.e. naturalised) who had settled since 1945. The state only became troubled when immigration became politicised in debates over citizenship and nationhood in the 1980s and 90s. (Kastoryano and Crowley, UNESCO-MOST) Up until then, the state aim was socio-economic insertion of immigrants focussed on jobs, housing and welfare, without concern for culture or religion. Although immigrants were mainly Muslim, this was not perceived as a problem. (Favell, 1998, 47) Almost three quarters of a million Algerians form 22% of the foreigner population with the Portuguese almost equal, with 21%, with 12% Moroccan, 9% Italian, 9% Spanish, 5% Turkish, 5% Tunisian, and 4% Central African. (Favell, 1998, 49) The new immigrants now come largely from North Africa, but also West Africa - the Ivory Coast and Senegal, and Madagaskar.

Two major shifts took place in civic republicanism in the 1980s, linked to the political divergence of left and right in immigration and integration policy. In the 1981 amnesty, the first Left government in the post-war period under Mitterrand, regularised the position of longstanding clandestine migrants shut out after the stop on immigration in the early 1970s and adopted a multicultural, pluralist stance. As the young generation of North Africans mobilised, '*beur*' identity became a badge of pride, expressed as the right to be different. In reality, they were claiming the right to be treated equally although they were culturally different, and the Left responded.

However the failure of its social and economic policy, with deindustrialisation and new ghettoes in the *banlieues* resulting from efforts at slum clearance, produced the reactive mobilisation of the racist Front National, and the reassertion of the right, with an ethnic revision of republicanism in competition with Le Pen.

The right-wing UDF/RPR coalition elected in 1986, attempted a new immigration control, clamping down on illegal residents and an end to *ius soli* for second generation born in France of foreign-born parents, as the Thatcher government had done in Britain in 1981. However it was forced to withdraw and set up a Commission on Nationality which reformulated a more individualist social contract, where nationality was no longer automatic, but the entitlement to register remained unconditional, along with *ius soli* - automatic nationality at birth to third generation children with at least one French parent, and easily accessible to second generation children with five years residence and no criminal record. For Algerian parents born before 1962 and thus considered French, their children were confirmed as French at birth. (Favell, 68)

Despite the logic of 'minorities' or 'communities' being rejected, typified by the refusal to collect ethnic data, the High Council reports on poverty and unemployment which responded to the social agitation of the 1980s began to collect data on country of origin of respondents and family form, giving a 'strong substantive idea of what culturally being French should be' and of non-French otherness. (*alterité*) However action on social integration proposed accommodation of Islam through promotion of association as a model for adapting religion to republican ideal, directing individuals to sanctioned organisations and public action.

An important source of change in the republican model has resulted from immigrant self-organisation and local community action, fostered by the Left through the Fund for Social Action (Fonds D'Action Sociale) in 1980-3, out of which an urban concept of citizenship as activism in civil society has grown. So the government was pressured into action to drastically increase budgets to fight exclusion in the *banlieues* from 1990. This activated civil society has also articulated its own cultural demands - not least in the infamous *l'affaire des foulards* when Muslim girls were sent home from school for wearing headscarfs. The girls argued an immaculate republican case in terms of their right to education as French citizens. Despite a racist campaign by the Front National with echoes in the media, the state was forced to reinstate them. (Gaspard and Khosrow-Khavar, 1995) Islamic voluntary associations, have also developed independently of state recognition but began to claim their presence in civil society. The state, because of its *laicité* had not previously acknowledged Islamic religious organisation as a public presence, tried at first to control Islamic political expression by setting up a Council of Reflection on Islam (CORIF) in 1990. However, the initiative was very unrepresentative and so in 1995 the state was forced to recognise the 'Representative Council of Muslims', on the same basis as the Representative Council of the Jews (CRIF) Not only has civil society become more pluralistic in the sense of active citizenship, but the state's integratory powers as guarantor of social cohesion have also been challenged.

While civic republicanism is laicist, and religion considered a private matter, the personal display of symbols of religious faith by Catholics (and by Jews), was tolerated in contrast to the episodes of intolerance by public authorities towards Muslim girls wearing headscarves to school. The recent outlawing by the Right under President Chirac of the wearing of signs of religious identity in school, covering Muslim headscarves, Sikh turbans, Jewish skullcaps and large crosses (!) has reasserted a strict, monocultural conception of the public domain, even at the expense of some young people's education. Cases are currently being contested in court by three Sikh boys excluded from school for wearing the turban.

The process of pluralising public culture was aided by the success of the French national team in the football World Cup in 1998 and in the European Championships in 2000. The key role played in these victories by French footballers of different ethnic origins like Zidane, Henry, Vieira and Djorkaeff enabled the Left in France to turn what could have been a traditional reassertion of national grandeur into a pluralistic redefinition of the nation. However, these symbolic changes have to some extent been reversed by the unfavourable international climate since 9/11 which has fed paranoia and Islamophobia, and by the ascendance of the French Republican Right.

Compared to Britain, the French civic tradition is better able to transcend neighbourhood-based, class and ethnic identities, and offer a stronger sense of shared belonging to the city. Such civic identification is especially important today, in times of growing social fragmentation. In France the civic space is highly prized, as evidenced by the quality of design, maintenance and access to the public realm e.g. the successful upgrading of public transport systems and public spaces in cities like Lyons and Strasbourg. The high quality of urban spaces and services is visible also in schemes for improving peripheral housing estates (*banlieues*) where there are high concentrations of immigrants, such as the Banlieues '89 project, led by architect Roland Castro, on behalf of President Mitterrand. At its most successful, it added a degree of civic urbanity to working-class dormitory areas, through the development of new squares, high quality housing, public art, cultural centres and festivals. (Castro, 1994)

The development of the public realm in France since the 1970s has encompassed many *grands projets*, mainly based in Paris, including the Pompidou Centre, the Louvre Pyramid and the Opera at La Bastille. The only example of an intercultural flagship project is the Institut du Monde Arabe, built through a partnership between the French government and forty-one countries in the Arab world. The Institute is an important symbol both of a more intercultural history of the French nation and its colonial relations and also of post-colonial collaboration between states, on the basis of mutual respect and an implicit critique of U.S.-dominated globalisation. It is an exemplary laboratory for intercultural experiment in education, research, art, crafts and design.

The 'Melting Pot' Approach and the Drift to Ethnic Essentialism: the U.S.

The U.S. melting pot approach shared with the French model civic integration through a common language and adherence to constitutional rights, while it differed as an immigrant and federal nation, in having implicit recognition of cultural diversity at local level. However, as it is more market-led, relying on individual advancement without the glue of high-grade social rights and public services, it has increasingly failed. Social inequalities have become entrenched especially in African American neighbourhoods with a serious erosion of ladders of opportunity and criminalisation of large sections of the black population as an underclass. The decline of the melting pot has been accelerated by the growth of Spanish as a contender to English as the dominant language. The response to this crisis have often been a form of ethnic essentialism, with the growth of highly segregated communities and ethnic and religious fundamentalisms.

This response is visible both among disadvantaged ethnic minority communities and affluent elites who increasingly favour gated and fortified "common interest developments" (CIDs) which take the form of privatised, cities within the city, providing for the needs of specific lifestyle groups, such as couples without children, large families, gays and lesbians.

Ethnic Nationalism and the *Gastarbeiter* System

This policy framework was underpinned in Germany by a strong ethnic conception of nationality which led not only to a denial of being a country of immigration, but to strong restrictions against naturalisation and hostility to multiculturalism. Cultural diversity (*kulturelle Vielfalt*) is understood exclusively in a territorial sense as the product of regional and local differences. This model not only applies to Germany but also Austria and was the predominant, though not exclusive influence on Belgium's immigration.

Germany

German nationalism in the 19th century had an ethno-linguistic concept of the nation, based on a common language and culture. The failure of unification to incorporate the majority of German speaking people in the state, reinforced the aspiration for ethno-cultural unity, so nationhood was legally expressed in terms of descent – *ius sanguinis* - rather than residence on the territory. (Brubaker, 1992) This ethnic conception of culture and state was perpetuated after the war, despite its racial connotations, to maintain the West German claim to East Germany.

The *Gastarbeiter* recruitment through bilateral agreements first with Italy and then in the 1960s with Spain, Greece, Turkey, Portugal and Yugoslavia was centrally organised by the Federal Labour Office, who screened and selected workers. The state treated them as an expendable workforce but with annual renewal of contracts by employers who found it uneconomic to recruit and train each year, they became a permanent presence. Under international law, dependents could join them. Consequently, the foreigner presence grew rapidly but fluctuated with recession. The 1973 November stop on primary migration, banned recruitment from non E.C. countries despite existing agreements but by then the migrant population had grown to 2.6 million. With subsequent family reunion, the total resident foreigner population increased to 4 million. Whereas migrants from the European Community countries like Italy, Spain and Greece, acquired equivalent status to Germans, second and third generation German-speaking Turks and Moroccans continued to be treated as foreigners without rights.

The German ethnic conception of culture expressed in the Constitution as *Volkszugehörigkeit* - belonging to the *Volk* – imposed many obstacles on naturalisation. You were required to prove long residence in suitable accommodation, a good reputation and lack of criminal record, the capacity to earn a living and support dependents and not rely on welfare, fluency in written and spoken language, voluntary attachment to Germany, a basic knowledge of the Constitution and commitment to Germany's basic order, so as to be able to satisfy a judge that would make 'a valuable contribution to German society'. (Hailbronner, 1989, 68)

Against the backdrop of unprecedented levels of racist violence after unification in 1991-2 directed at both asylum seekers and immigrants, and internal political concern about German's European image, the law was gradually reformed. The 1991 new Aliens Law set out eligibility for naturalisation of foreigners who renounced their previous citizenship and met formal residence requirements, removing the prejudicial requirement to prove extraordinary loyalty to German culture and constitutional order although authorisation was still subject to bureaucratic discretion and *ius sanguinis* remained in force. The law still barred Turks who could not renounce their Turkish citizenship without losing property rights. In 1993 though, naturalisation became a legal right following 15 years residence, still the longest requirement in Europe. However it was not until 2001 that *ius soli*, birth on the territory was written into citizenship law and dual citizenship was allowed, thus resolving the longstanding exclusion of Turks from citizenship status and voting rights.

As access to social welfare in Germany does not depend on citizenship, the minority population was relatively well treated socially although the degree and scope of entitlement varied according to foreigner status, privileging ethnic Germans over asylum seekers and Turks. (Kvistad, 1998, 147-8) Many immigrants were beneficiaries of social housing although the state curtailed provision in the 1990s that has adversely affected refugees. However, no special language provision was made until the 1990s and Turks in particular have been blamed for their poor German.

Proponents of post-nationalism have argued that Turks acquired equivalent economic and social entitlements to German citizens through international law and human rights. (Soysal 1994) However the lack of formal citizenship for the longest period, affecting three generations, helps to account for the cultural marginalisation of these minorities in Germany. In addition to the substantial racial and anti-Islamic stereotyping of Turks, Moroccans and Arabs as fundamentalist, backward-looking and ghettoised, which is not unique to Germany but particularly marked in countries with *Gastarbeiter* regimes, minority cultures are still treated as foreign and traditional or exotic and their artists as ambassadors for their country of origin. This view denies their contemporary relevance and presence in German society and discourages the wider population from cultural interaction. Such an outlook was summed up in the political defence of the purity of Germany culture as the 'leading culture' (*Leitkultur*) by the Christian Democrat right as recently as 2001. (Bloomfield, 2003)

Since 1998, the German Social Democratic government has moved away from an ethnically essentialist nationality law which denies rights and recognition to 2nd, 3rd and now 4th generation Turks, Arabs and other immigrants as German citizens. Although they were born in Germany, have their home there and speak German as their first language, they were not recognized as new kinds of German. The nationality law has hampered the acknowledgement of the *de facto* multicultural character of German society and made it more difficult to curb the high levels of racial violence against 'foreigners'. This has been a lost opportunity to renew German culture, recognising the cultural contribution of ethnic minorities and the new cultural hybrids which are emerging. (Bloomfield, 2001) Nevertheless, because of the federal nature of the German state, key cities such as Berlin and Frankfurt, have developed autonomous policy experiments which have encouraged the social integration of ethnic minorities, forms of political participation and cultural recognition. Some of these experiments verge on adopting an intercultural practice. (Bloomfield, 2003; Vertovec, 1995; Sandercock,1998, 139-45)

The Southern European approach: from laissez-faire unregulated regime to a restrictive regime as countries of new immigration

Italy, Spain and Portugal were countries of emigration up until the 1980s and so immigration was literally unregulated and undocumented, with fairly relaxed naturalisation procedures. In Spain and Portugal, children of foreigners born on the territory could obtain nationality with 5 years residence. In Italy there was a five-year residency requirement for naturalisation. Increasing demand for cheap labour to fill niches in the manufacturing economy and for domestics to provide care in the home grew and so did the economic crisis in Africa which made temporary and seasonal migration more permanent.

The Southern European states then shifted gear suddenly to highly restrictive immigration regimes, high profile clampdowns on clandestine immigration, with periodic amnesties under Left governments and local ad hoc integration initiatives, dependent on the political colour of the local government, but without establishing a firm legal footing for immigration or integration. Under European Union pressure to close the southern border of Europe to Africa, and to integrate immigration and asylum policies under the Schengen agreement, the Southern Europeans imposed visa requirements, imposed fines on airlines carrying undocumented migrants, and raised the residency qualification for naturalisation from five years to ten years.

As countries of emigration – their own inhabitants migrated from the south to northern Europe in the 1950s and 60s post-war boom. Domestically rural labour moved to the towns to higher productivity sectors of the economy but the by 1970s these countries were themselves experiencing labour shortages which pushed up wages for the indigenous workforce. Cheaper labour was imported to fill niches in dirty manual jobs in the foundries and car factories that the indigenous would no longer do. (King and Black, 1997) However, the declining rate of investment and restructuring in manufacturing created new unemployment among the immigrant workforce.

The crisis in Africa in the 1980s-1990s led to new migration to Spain, Portugal and Italy of more permanent street sellers who formed co-operatives and came into conflict with indigenous traders. The demise of welfare provision also led to the growth of domestics – mainly Filipino women to Italy and Spain, organised through the Catholic Church.

Italy

Debate in Italy focussed heavily on exclusion and clandestine migration with the aim of sealing the border with scant regard for the social situation of the immigrants. With the exception of small Ethiopian, Eritrean and Somalian communities resulting deriving from colonial links, migration to Italy has been characterised by the lack of linguistic and cultural ties and sexual segregation rather than family reunion. There has been almost exclusively male migration from North and West Africa and the sub Continent, and exclusively female migration from the Philippines, Cape Verde and the Ivory Coast. At first, seasonal and temporary in nature, and often in transit to Northern Europe, it has only recently become a permanent settlement and so there is not as yet a second generation.

The legislative framework for immigration and integration was not firmly established and still lurches from left to right, from integration to expulsion. The Martelli bill in 1990 gave amnesty to clandestine immigrants who had entered Italy before December 1989, yet despite the comprehensive character of the legislation, in 1995 the Right introduced the Nespoli law which made illegal entry a criminal offence, with detention and expulsion of undocumented immigrants. In 1998 with the advent of the Centre Left government, the Napolitano-Turco law put immigration on a legal footing, establishing entitlements to health care, education, social housing, protection against discrimination, the right to sponsor the immigration of a relative and to participate in local elections.

However the advent of the second Berlusconi government has brought forward the Bossi-Fini law which goes a long way to closing the borders to asylum seekers and criminalising immigrants by requiring they be fingerprinted, lengthening the required stay from five to six years before a non-EU immigrant can qualify for legal residence, making re-entry of foreigners who have been expelled within the last 12 years a criminal offence, punishable with imprisonment. Already in 2001, the government reported that 42,100 migrants had been expelled. (World Refugee Survey 2003) It prevents family reunion of disabled relatives, except children. In order to regularise their situation, domestics in families now have to pay a tax. The government also holds asylum seekers in detention centres for initial decisions ostensibly up to 30 days but in 2002 this procedure took 12-15 months and has also complicated the right of appeal against deportation and reduced the time to lodge an appeal from 60 to 5 days.

In this climate of government hostility, the discretionary power of the administration is encouraged to obstruct. So naturalisation which immigrants become eligible for after ten years, can be delayed way beyond, as has been the case of a Senagalese actor in our study, Modou Gueye, who has been waiting thirteen years to become a citizen. (Modou Gueye, Interview with Jude Bloomfield, 2003)

However, as in Spain and particularly Portugal, the political autonomy of local and regional government has enabled strong city and voluntary initiatives, stemming from the Catholic Church, particularly in small cities in the old red belt in Central Italy, such as Modena, Reggio Emilia, Ravenna and Arezzo which have provided immigrant reception and settlement, language training, job placement, integrated schooling and cultural programmes, including festivals. (Hellman, 1997, 39) The region of Tuscany and the city of Turin stand out for their intercultural initiatives, through the Porto Franco Intercultura project and the Intercultural Centre in Turin. These have begun to integrate the diverse migration and minority presence in the region into regional history and disseminate interculturalism through library-learning centres, exhibitions, teaching, joint cultural production and festivals. Rome City Council has invested money to help poor immigrants regularise by paying their taxes, establishing an official register of care assistants and paying for the inexperienced young women to qualify. (Gianguido Palumbo, Interview with Jude Bloomfield, 2003)

Spain
In the 1960s, Spain and Portugal had experienced a trickle individual artists and students migrating – mainly from Latin America but not migration of groups. As former colonial powers – their migrants came mainly from former colonies, so they had a language in common. But Spain did not form a cultural community with her ex-colonies although it did facilitate citizenship for Latin Americans and Filipinos, requiring only 2 years legal residence to naturalise and gain the vote instead of 10 years. (Morén-Alegret, 2002, 93)

Under Spanish law three regularisations took place in 1985-6, 1991 and 1996 under left pressure, but Socialist government only produced non-statutory guidelines for regularisation according to the needs of the labour market and 'absorption capacity', along with social and economic aid to countries of origin and expulsion of undocumented workers. In 1996 they set up an Inter-Ministry Commission on

Immigration to coordinate action across departments and tighten procedures. In 1991 they imposed visas on immigrants from Morocco, Tunisia, Algeria, Peru, then the Dominican Republic. By 1995 the number of countries requiring visas had risen to over 130 along with a new restrictive Asylum Act, even though the proportion of migrants in the Spanish population remained very low at 1.2%. Less than 20% of these were from Africa, the biggest group among them being Moroccans, and 25% came from Latin America – especially Argentina.

With the exclusionary thrust of new regulations, they were forced to recognise associational rights to immigrants and were pressured to undertake social integration measures. In 1993 Migration Office drew up a General Immigration Plan for Social Integration which set up an Immigrant Forum for exchange with voluntary organisations and an observatory to research and monitor minority ethnic groups. The Government also fixed quotas of migrants from different nationalities in different economic sectors but used them to regularise immigrant status. However with the Conservative government since 1996 expulsions were resumed and policy focus switched back from integration to exclusion of poor country migrants, and border control.

Portugal
Post-colonisation Portugal experienced a rapid burst of immigration from Africa – Cape Verde, Mozambique, Angola, Guinea Bissau, plus East Timor and Goa and after 1986 also strong migration from European Community countries to Lisbon where 55% of all migrants lived (1995 figure). Despite the influx, the migrant population in Portugal in 1995 was also comparatively low at 1.7%, almost half from Africa, especially Cape Verde and about a quarter from Latin America mainly Brazil. It has sought to develop 'Lusufonia' like Francophonie, a privileged cultural community with its ex-colonies, with preferential terms of naturalisation and citizenship for those who migrate but this came into conflict with the pressures for Fortress Europe.

The new nationality law 37/1981 reversed the previous open attitude and abandoned the principle of *ius soli*, so depriving children who were born in Portugal of non-Portuguese parents of citizenship. Although the Constitution was revised to recognise the status of foreigner in Portugal, this was aimed at EU citizens rather than African immigrants. Naturalisation was also made harder in 1994 by raising the residence requirement to six years for the privileged group of post-colonial migrants and from five years to ten years for migrants from elsewhere. (Moreen-Alegret, 2002) Another cultural operator in our study, who is Brazilian, Tela Laeo has been waiting eleven years to naturalise, setting up a small business which is Portuguese, allowing her to trade in the EU whereas she is not. (Tela Laeo, Interview with Jude Bloomfield, 13.7.03)

However, a campaign by left parties and immigrant associations for regularisation and an end to employers' withholding contracts was mounted in 1992-3 so the Conservative government acted to regularise and implement an integration programme of education, work training and information for immigrants but without engaging in dialogue with immigrants associations. The LusoAfrican youth movement mobilised politically in 1995 against the racial murder of an asylum seeker, demanding regularisation and cultural respect. (Albuquerque, 1999) The new Socialist government in 1995 enacted a second regularisation of foreigners in 1996 and a third one in 1999 covering non-Lusophone immigrants. It also embarked on a serious social policy for ethnic minorities, setting up a High Commissioner for Immigration and Ethnic Minorities (ACIME) directly under the Prime Minister, to co-ordinate policy across government departments, ensuring gypsies as well as immigrants were given special consideration in housing, education and employment. Despite this shift to social integration, there was no policy change on external immigration control or arrests and expulsion under Schengen. Nevertheless, the political system remained free of racism unlike Spain and Italy.

At local level in Lisbon, the promotion of integration under the Socialists had important cultural effects. The Municipal Council of Immigrant Communities and Ethnic Minorities, set up as a consultative body to the council, defended ethnic minority rights, respect for minority culture and identity and intercultural dialogue. It helped organise small local cultural festivals with immigrant associations even when its advisory role to the city was ended. Although an administrative body, the Ethnic Minorities Office, replaced it within Lisbon council, this was headed by a Mozambican artist, Inaçio Matinshe, who established a Multicultural Carnival in 1998 on the lines of a Lusuphone street carnival, with the participation of the post-colonial, immigrant organisations. (Morén-Alegret, 2002)

Transculturalism

This approach, promoted by UNESCO, is based on conceptions of global ethics and global citizenship. Strategies for cultural pluralism are based on goals which seek to transcend cultural differences through values which define and unify us as a species i.e. peace, solidarity, human rights, environmental sustainability, global justice. These should find embodiment in the symbols of the city centre, flagship buildings, public art, education and public awareness-raising programmes, transport, library and information services and social policies.

This approach is not new. It gained momentum after the Second World War with the development of peace memorials and gardens, and of the town twinning movement. In its more traditional forms, transculturalism can produce anodyne or banal solutions which unconsciously fall back on monocultural traditions which are assumed to be universal, but have not engaged in an intercultural process.

The acceleration of globalisation processes and the world environmental crisis have given new impetus to transcultural initiatives such the Local Agenda 21 movement and global citizenship education programmes aimed at young people, such as the Birmingham Youth Parliament project and the scheme recently launched by Turin City Council in preparation for the city's hosting of the winter Olympics in 2006. (*I ragazzi del 2006*) Another example is the Universal Forum of Cultures, held between May and September 2004 in Barcelona, an initiative developed by Barcelona City Council in co-operation with the Catalan and Spanish governments and UNESCO. It was intended to be the first of a series of programmes to be held every four years in different cities across the world. The first Forum included exhibitions, performances, conferences and debates focussed on transcultural themes, involving most countries around the globe. (see www.barcelona2004.org). The next Forum will take place in Monterrey in 2007.

However transculturalism is problematic for artists, designers, planners and policy makers to achieve. They are embedded in particular cultures and can only address universal needs and aspirations which cut across all cultures from the imaginary thrown up by their own particular professional and personal cultural mix. Yet, as we have shown, universalism is best achieved through a process of intercultural exchange, drawing on commonalities between cultures and integrating and fusing elements of different traditions. So the cosmopolitan reimagining of the city is more likely to succeed through diversifying the cultural range of planners, architects, designers and artists commissioned, fostering intercultural collaboration between them and including diverse cultural traditions within the brief.

The argument we have put forward includes elements of civic integration and opening up multiculturalism beyond cultural boundaries, to develop intercultural overlap and wider dialogue. Transcultural initiatives would remain a symbolic, global affirmation of a common humanity, ecology and cosmos and therefore, are not the main basis of a transformation of everyday life in cities. An intercultural practice throughout urban policy offers a better hope than both cultural integrationist and multicultural models, as it does not seek to integrate 'others' into a given order but to remake the civic culture and public sphere so they reflect the diversity of the city and its citizens.

PART THREE

Examples of Best Practice: Intercultural Initiatives at City Level

Addressing Social and Economic Inequalities

Globalisation has exacerbated inequalities across the world between north and south and within post-industrial societies between those with secure employment and the 'flexible' insecure workforce in which ethnic minorities, women and young people figure prominently. Since the early 1980s the urban labour market has tended to polarise, between those better paid, skilled and more secure jobs in technical, managerial and professional fields and those in low paid, lesser skilled, often part-time occupations mainly in the service sector. Neo-liberal policies by national governments have led to cutbacks, reductions in access and growing privatisation of public services.

Intercultural policy responses have to aim to counter inequalities, without reinforcing ethnic divides, by reversing discrimination and exclusion trends. To do this they should be based on an analysis of needs, wherever they emerge, including in pockets of white working class deprivation. Informal skills, knowledge and other untapped resources also need to be identified. Part of the task of countering inequalities is to recognise that the misrecognition and undervaluing of ethnic minority cultures contributes to startling forms of social injustice, such as levels of black exclusions from school or the compulsory sectioning of black mental health patients and also represents a serious waste of opportunities.

The *Challenges for the Future* report, which came out of Birmingham's bold initiative to respond to the recommendations of the Macpherson inquiry, provides an invaluable snapshot of ethnic inequality in the city, in education, the labour market and training and proposes measures to monitor and counter discrimination, to ensure access for ethnic minorities and representation in key agencies in charge of local economic development strategies. However, it does not focus adequately on ethnic minority enterprise development. There is no analysis of the specific contributions of ethnic minorities to the different sectors of the local economy, and no discussion of how to tap their transnational connections to attract inward investment and skilled personnel.

The data shows that 28.7% of those entering self-employment under the Single Regeneration Budget (SRB) Challenge Fund in Birmingham between 1995-2000 were from black and minority ethnic backgrounds. However there are no data about what type of businesses are being set up. The report is weak in terms of proposals on business training and technical support which are needed to respond to this growth of self-employment and small business, particularly in the light of the greater difficulties that ethnic minorities face in accessing business support and regeneration grants, highlighted by Oc (in Carley, ed., 2000). The Custard Factory provides an example of what could be offered, yet its links with city government are weak.

The arts, crafts, electronic media and IT are among the main sectors young people want to work in and can also provide significant employment growth. Diverse sources of 'cultural 'capital (Bourdieu, 1977, 1984, 1992) in street and youth sub cultures, such the informal know-how developed in the club scene, from scratch and synthesising DJing (Thornton, 1995) are strongly developed among Black and Asian youth. Yet they have not been built upon in Birmingham, through the provision of rehearsal space, music industry training, recording studios, radio stations (according to the Black Cultural Forum established by Birmingham Race Action Partnership, interview with Lorna Shaw, 20.12.01.). The skills and networks acquired informally need to be linked in Birmingham to more formal training, to offer black and minority ethnic young people opportunities to develop their creative capacities and turn them to economic advantage in self-employment or micro businesses.

The Chocolate Factory – a centre of cultural micro enterprise and small business in Haringey, North London, established through an arts trust of members, brings together a range of culturally diverse businesses rather as the Custard Factory does, but on a smaller scale. One of its small companies, Ambitious Productions promotes Bhangra rock and is the major distributor in the UK of British Asian funk. It also makes and distributes videos as well as lending video equipment. (Venod Mitra, interview with Jude Bloomfield,1999) Interesting initiatives have begun in the music sector in Birmingham with Pato Banton's studio at Matthew Boulton College and U.B. 40's partnership with South Birmingham College to establish a studio in Eastside. However, these developments have not been fully integrated into local economic development and training strategies. A rare example of training targetted at Black and Asian cultural aptitudes and business needs is the Chocolate Factory's certificated training courses in music business, sound engineering and photography where 90 per cent of the students come from ethnic minorities.

The approach taken in *Challenges for the Future* tends to be reactive and focussed on public sector institutions and urban policies. It does not engage sufficiently with the raw material of entrepreneurial ideas, resources and networks in the city, and with the obstacles to capitalising on them fully.

In the small and medium-sized business sector, ethnic businesses have utilised diasporic networks and cultural specialisms and filled niches, like the Balti restaurant phenomenon in Birmingham. They, nonetheless, find themselves excluded from the key channels for allocating contracts. This has become a serious mechanism of exclusion, especially since contractualisation has spread to the public sector. This is a new kind of inequality that the ethnic business sector has begun to organise over – as reflected in the agendas of organisations like the Black Londoners' Forum and the Leicester Asian Business Association. The Government Office for the West Midlands has begun to address this problem by establishing links with the Asian and African Caribbean business networks, to support capacity building among ethnic minority businesses. (*Challenges for the Future*, 2001, 25) Chambers of Commerce and one-stop agencies for attracting inward investment need to become much more attuned to the opportunities for transnational networking offered by diasporic business communities – particularly links with India and China.

a. Culturally Informed Local Economic Development Initiatives:

Undervaerket, Randers in Denmark
The Undervaerket regeneration project in Randers, Denmark is a local economic development initiative, located in an area of traditional industrial decline (Ostergade) with a high concentration of ethnic minorities. Although this is an employment-driven initiative, its strength lies in the way it combines regeneration, job creation, training, small business support and tourism agenda harnessing cultural diversity to a cultural industries strategy. It is creating a regional centre of arts and crafts, with a 'bazaar' style market incorporating ethnic shops and services such as a Turkish bakery, hairdressing salon and Turkish bath, (the first in Denmark) a handicrafts shop, training workshops in glass-blowing, textile printing and weaving, a gallery showcasing and selling tapestries made by Turkish and Tamil women, a puppet theatre and auditoriun for music and theatre. The educational and training facilities are targetted at

ethnic minorities and run by a training organisation Kulturkaelderen which specialises in programmes for migrants and refugees. As well as vocational training in construction for the long-term unemployed, leading to subsidised placements in building firms and then some permanent jobs, there is also training in business start-up, covering business planning, accounting, marketing, IT and language. (www.undervaerket.dk/; ERDF Urban Pilot programme: (www.inforegio.cec.eu.int/urban/upp/SRC/frame1.htm)

Spitalfields and Brick Lane, East London
The development of the Brick Lane area and the battle over Spitalfields market also highlight important characteristics of building inter-ethnic alliances and the strategic capacity of marginalised people to intervene in planning decisions that affect their livelihood. It also indicates the power of ethnic small business when mobilised to prevent being trampled on by large-scale property developers. Spitalfields area, a traditional point of entry and settlement for immigrants, has a highly permeable and productive structure of small workshops and family firms in the rag trade.

The area is very mixed, marked by successive waves of migration, once predominantly Jewish and now Bangladeshi and Indian, attracting skilled artisans and street traders, and more recently young designers and artists. When the workshops came under great pressure from the late 1970s for upgrading under threat of closure or unaffordable rent rises, a number of small businesses banded together in the Spitalfields Small Business Association to buy out the old landlords. They drew on their own political and cultural traditions of mutual support and pooling resources to establish a co-op, which modernised and improved the workshops and rented them back to the tenants at a non-profit rent. Gradually they bought up hundreds of workshops to secure the economic future of the area. They have gone on to develop a cultural business strategy for Brick Lane as Banglatown, with upgraded restaurants, shops and craft workspaces to attract visitors to the area. (Brick Lane Business Association manifesto)

In reaction to pressure from the property developers who sought to extend, the boundary of the financial City from Broadgate into Spitalfields, the Community Development Group – an umbrella of sixty community organisations - managed to form a unified voice. It formulated a Community Plan in 1989 which integrated social housing with training and literacy needs of the area. It worked with sympathetic community planners in the design of housing and streets to meet the need for security and proximity of the Bengali community and developed a capacity to negotiate directly with developers and the planning authority.

In property boom of the late 1980s, it managed to intervene to prevent the developers and Corporation of London from destroying the Spitalfields Market. Although they could not prevent the closure of the fruit and vegetable market which helped keep rateable values down and rents low, they successfully used a Planning Gain Agreement to acquire £5 million from the developers which went into a Community Development Trust. The developer collapsed in the property boom crash, relieving the pressure on the area for a time. The Trust was able to develop a strategy for the short-term use of the market to support local businesses and independent traders in the hope of safeguarding the local economy from future encroachment from the corporate sector. It diversified uses and public –providing restaurants, a mobile opera house to visitors, tennis courts to serve City workers during their lunchbreaks, and a Sunday market including crafts and organic produce.

In the renewed threat to the market from the Spitalfields Development Group's plan to demolish the western end of the market and build 600,000 sq ft. of offices for the City, an even broader alliance has been formed including faith communities and environmentalists. SMUT – the Spitalfields Market Under Threat campaign has extended the alliance to the Anglican churches of the East End and the East London Mosque, the Civic Trust and the Environmental Trust. This should not be seen as an ethnic struggle of Bengalis, or even Bengali small business but one based on alliances with the old East End Cockney traders in Petticoat Lane, radical white middle class planners and community activists, and conservationists in Spitalfields Historic Buildings Trust concerned to protect the Georgian conservation area. The alliance in the Community Development Trust was on a crucial learning curve which broadened horizons, making participants aware of the needs of others in the area. It is highly unlikely that they would have been as successful as they have been, adjacent to the most costly real estate in the world, had they not developed such a strategic capacity to marry needs and agree priorities so that they could act in a unified way. (Hugo Hinsley, interview with Jude Bloomfield, 12. 12. 01. For an alternative view see: Sandercock, 1998, 170-171;

www.eastendlife.com /crt/fun_bricklane.shtml; www.smut.org.uk/)

b. Culturally Diverse Approaches to Health: South Birmingham

In 1993, Constituency Action Teams were set up in south Birmingham in response to the Bosanquet Report profiling Birmingham's primary healthcare problems. The Regional Health Authority came up with an unexpectedly large sum of money, £20 million to fund the initiatives to regain credibility after closing a number of hospitals in the city. The local inter-agency response, rare at the time, sought local community-based solutions to defined health problems.

One such scheme in Sparkhill, for Community Parents, sought to address the very high infant, perenatal and accident mortality in a predominantly Asian area, identifying a breakdown in generational transmission of knowledge of neo-natal care. By operating on the principle that experienced mothers in poor communities could give practical support to inexperienced mothers who were struggling to cope with their newborn infants, a scheme was set up to train local women, combining local and health authority funding with SRB and European Integra programme finance earmarked for training ethnic minorities for jobs in areas where they are underrepresented. Many of the thirty two participants in the scheme were new entrant Pakistani women who had never been out of the house before, and did not speak English. They trained partly through working in the community and partly through doing a health and social care NVQ to level 2 or 3 at Joseph Chamberlain College. Although they could not enter the public sector under EU training rules, they set up a successful community business Compare (Community Parents) which is still operating. In this way, the strengths and skills of local women were channelled into solving a local health problem, and at the same time, severely ethnically disadvantaged women were able to access training and find a route into the labour market. However, the impact of the initiative on infant mortality in the area has not been fully evaluated. (Cynthia Bower, Assistant Director Social Services at the time and chair of Northfield Constituency Action Team, now head of Birmingham Specialist Community Health Trust, interview with Jude Bloomfield, 22.12.01.)

Birmingham Specialist Community Health Trust recently came third in the British Diversity Awards for its pioneering work in addressing and representing culturally diverse health needs and creating new routes of recruitment for ethnic minorities to health and welfare services. It set up in 1998 a Minority Ethnic Group Council to establish a forum for ethnic minorities and faith communities to identify local health needs and deficits and contribute to shaping services. One of the most interesting initiatives undertaken has been a training and employment partnership with two black voluntary sector organisations - Future Care and Ashram Housing, to train their young African-Caribbean and Asian volunteers and offer them employment in the Learning Disabilities Directorate, having discovered a surfeit of volunteers who were not being recruited through formal channels to the NHS. (Birmingham Specialist Community Health NHS Trust, 2001.)

Counteracting Ethnic Segregation in Urban Space

Settlement patterns in cities through the operation of the housing market, past zoning policies and voluntary clustering of communities have often interacted to produce socially and culturally segregated areas. Ladders for social mobility, especially for newly arrived immigrants, have been undermined with intensified economic and ethnic polarisation, particularly in some old inner urban areas and peripheral housing estates which suffer multiple deprivation. These neighbourhoods are fundamental places of social interaction for local residents but largely because they are trapped there, with a sense that there is no way out. This can lead to unrest, vandalism and other destructive behaviour, but also in some cases, to new forms of youth culture distinguished by an aesthetics of speed, danger, violence and immediacy. (Bianchini and Santacatterina, 1997, 41)

It has also led to a process of stigmatisation of these areas. This is reflected in the behaviour of employers, the police, the media and potential house buyers. Even in the cases where some of these areas have been gentrified, middle class white parents often remove their children from schools where poorer ethnic minority children are concentrated. In some cases, local residents themselves react to this stigmatisation by declining to use neighbourhood facilities in their free time, preferring to get out. (Bianchini and Santacatterina,1997, 70-2) As a result of these processes, poverty has often come to be seen as 'ethnic', as a culturally transmitted stigma rather than being based on adverse social and economic circumstances.

Socially and culturally mixed areas do not spontaneously emerge but require imaginative and carefully balanced planning. Birmingham City Council's policy, outlined in Highbury 3, aims to devolve service delivery to the neighbourhoods. If done at too small a scale to enable diversity, this could hinder efforts to counteract segregationist trends. (Rogers, 2000). The *Challenges for the Future* report also highlights low levels of black and ethnic minority staff in Birmingham City Council's planning, environmental services, transport and housing departments which makes it more difficult to deploy these key services to tackle ethnic segregation in the city.

City policy-makers can create 'soft boundaries' where people go outside their normal segregated experience and share a common space, within which social and cultural interaction and overlap takes place. In order to achieve this, it is important to have at the centre of urban planning and design strategies the notion of the city as a network of public spaces and as a system of interconnected parts.

In some cases, market-driven urban strategies have led to a reorientation of planning towards the design of customised, separate micro environments with virtually no communication between them and little attention to the 'spaces in between.' In the case of Birmingham, a strategy of interconnectedness and permeability is needed, particularly in view of the fact that the city grew up, incorporating 'villages' which have now become neighbourhoods with distinctive social and ethnic characteristics.

One example of good practice is provided by the public space strategy implemented by Barcelona City Council since the second half of the 1980s, which has involved the creation of many new public squares, pedestrian routes, neighbourhood parks, small open air theatres, punctuated with artworks including mosaics, sculptures and fountains. The strategy aimed both to provide new focal points for social aggregation and identity in neighbourhoods and to create linkages through public space between the peripheral areas, the city centre and the seafront. The achievement of this latter objective has been compromised by the failure to integrate the strategy adequately with traffic reduction measures. (Landry *et.al,* 1996)

a. Creating Soft Boundaries through Parks: *Clissold Park*, North London, and *Cannon Hill Park,* Birmingham.
Strategically placed parks - with a wide range of activities – sport, conservation and wildlife, natural history education, and a programme

of cultural animation and festivals provide one such meeting-place for shared cultural experience. (Greenhalgh and Worpole, 1995, 67) Clissold Park in London which lies between upwardly mobile professional Highbury and the multicultural mixed area of Stoke Newington in Hackney, are such examples. The latter has football pitches, a children's park, tennis courts, wildlife ponds, a small farm and aviary, a cheap cheerful café open 365 days of the year, a stage, and programme of activities managed by conservation and user groups. On visits to this park, you come across people from mental health hostels relaxing on benches, Asian women in saris playing football, Chassidic fathers playing with daughters, Orthodox Muslims in kaftans kicking around a football with their boys, men strolling with prams, mixed groups playing chess. It holds a range of festivals - from Cuban music to the homeless festival of scrap metal art. Cannon Hill Park between Balsall Heath and Edgbaston similarly operates as a soft boundary, with wide use of the park by Asian families and the white professional middle classes, and of the Midlands Arts Centre, which includes a café, bar and cinema and runs an attractive programme of intercultural activities, especially for children.

b. Siting of Cultural Infrastructure and Meeting Places

The siting of social and cultural infrastructure such as swimming pools and parks, clubs and cultural centres is important to facilitate everyday meeting and exchange between people of different backgrounds and neighbourhoods. The location of such facilities can play an important part in enabling the sharing of common spaces even where groups or friends remain in their own circles. Common spaces create a context then for shared association – for example of environmental user groups, mother and toddler groups and festivals in parks or casual lounging and chatting, training and children's parties in swimming pools which are mixed. Amin rightly stresses the importance of repeated social encounter of a routine kind – in schools, colleges, youth centres and sports clubs, and of alternative spaces of 'banal transgression' offering new cultural experiences which unsettle fixed identities and relationships. (Amin, 2002) He cites communal multiethnic ventures such as youth projects, shared childcare initiatives, communal gardens, regeneration of derelict spaces as initiatives that create popular experience of negotiating differences that build confidence in the capacity to solve problems and a sense of shared fate.

Birmingham, like many other multicultural cities suffers from the fact that dance clubs are highly segregated on lines of ethnicity and musical genre. The location of arts venues such as Birmingham's Drum arts centre and cinemas showing Bollywood movies in ethnic minority neighbourhoods deprives them of the opportunity of attracting wider mixed audiences and also, marginalises their cultural impact on the city. This also prevents these cultural centres from transforming the monocultural atmosphere of the city centre.

One solution is to locate re-founded, intercultural arts and media venues in city centres. For example the plan for the **Leicester Cultural Quarter** in the St. George's area of the city centre includes a new home for the Haymarket Theatre, which intends to make cultural diversity more integral to their recruitment, management, programming and marketing policies. There are also proposals to create an attractive and pedestrian-friendly route between the cultural quarter and the Peepul centre, a new intercultural flagship arts and community centre currently being built in the Belgrave area, in the heart of the city's Hindu communities. (see www.peepul.centre.com)

Another possible solution is to adopt a very aggressive marketing strategy to promote peripheraly located venues in order to achieve a city-wide appeal. For this to happen, the programming of the venues needs to become more mixed and intercultural. One good example of this is provided by **the 'Culture Network' strategy implemented by Vienna City Council** for programming and marketing of its neighbourhood centres. The strategy guarantees an integrated programming across the city so that each neighbourhood centre in the course of the year offers events which attract people from other parts of the city, of different social and ethnic backgrounds. (Bianchini and Santacatterina, 1997, 94)

One of the most striking examples of the importance of the physical siting of cultural projects was offered by the **Apelarte youth arts project in Loures** in Portugal. Apelarte was a multicultural youth arts project linked to a community development and housing project in Quinta da Fonte, 'Fountain Farm' district of Loures, a town on the outskirts of Lisbon. It houses a small, poor, very young multicultural community, with 90% on supplementary income support and half under the age of 15, 40% of whom are Portuguese African, 40% gypsy, and 20% Portuguese.

Apelarte, an adjunct to a Community Development project which dealt with health education and childcare, worked on a number of principles common to successful culturally diverse youth arts projects. It used professional artists and high-quality facilities across a range of art forms which reflected the young people's cultural traditions. Set in a non-institutional environment, it employed a workshop format as a means to overcome young people's disaffection from school while offering the cognitive tools and training to enable them to undertake their own projects and gain confidence in making their own professional and life choices. Apelarte gave free access to computers, photography, video, African dance, gypsy and Portuguese music, sculpture, theatre, and sports in well-equipped facilities including a cinema, library, exhibition hall and auditorium.

The facilities were based in the Municipal House of Culture which is strategically located between the old part of the town and the newer migrant districts quarters of Quinta da Fonte. According to the project leader, Cristina Santhinho, this location "made integration and intercultural dialogue much easier". (Santhinho 2000, 5)

The project was also innovative in the new links it made with the school through the 'school guidance action' which provided help with homework and literacy and through pedagogic clubs in school which integrated Apelarte activities such as photography and video into the school curriculum. It also spread the effects by establishing a local animateurs' club of youth street leaders who organised informal groups to run a football tournament or disseminate info to young people at risk.

In this way it encouraged intergenerational, as well as intercultural, dialogue. The collective celebration of the independence days of Angola, Mozambique, Guinea Bissau and of Gypsy Day and the formation of a multicultural choir brought mutual forms of cultural recognition and respect. The combination of anti-exclusion strategies and strategic siting both helped to combat ethnic segregation. Unfortunately this experiment was closed down but it remains a significant example of an imaginative intercultural and intergenerational approach and ethos that can be applied elsewhere.

c. Countering ethnic stigmatisation through place marketing: Hyson Green
The Hyson Green district of Nottingham is a stigmatised neighbourhood which has successfully implemented a place

marketing strategy to counter the stigma of poverty, racism and crime, under the campaign slogan "Life at the heart of the city". It focussed on the history and cultural richness of the area and residents' express perceptions of its tolerance, easy-going atmosphere and mix of cultures - the wide range of specialist shops, ethnic foods and fabrics - as well as its closeness to the city centre, and highlight annual event - the Goose Fair – to change its negative image. The media campaign used a wide range of initiatives including banner adverts in the Nottingham Evening Post, posters on buses and sites throughout the city, a photographic competition recording positive aspects of everyday life in the area which was exhibited afterwards and a website showcasing the cultural diversity of the area, with a news section and business portal. A series of highly publicised promotional events, such as a public food-tasting in the market square, a specially produced Hyson Green tea launched at a Tea Dance and a 'Life at the Heart' CD featuring music tracks and lyrics by local school students were key to experiencing the area differently.

The project, funded by the ERDF's URBAN Programme in 2000 to 2002 with an initial £100,000 budget, appears from the evaluation, to have impacted on the consciousness of residents and outsiders, attracting commercial investors and new homeowners to the area. (www.life-at-the-heart.co.uk/ hyson.htm)

d. Information technology and communication strategies to develop intercultural contact and place attachment: *Aston Pride*
Plans for extending access to information technology with digital link-ups across cities appear to offer great possibilities for cultural diversity strategies connecting marginalized groups to the society, enhancing participation and 'e.democracy.' It is easy to be mesmerised by the technology into thinking that in itself it will build up the cultural capital of information-poor people. There are numerous projects which have incorporated IT access into broader regeneration schemes such as the Gate in Turin, (see below) or are running limited experiments to test out specific social effects such as Telematic Naples. This is setting up telematic recreation centres in two piazze in contrasting areas, one city-centre based with an ageing and declining population, the other in the eastern periphery of Ponticelli, with a young population, plus a network of telematic kiosks providing free information about city services, traffic and cultural events and also commercial listings. So the project is designed to facilitate

generational access to communication technologies, rather than addressing cultural diversity as such. (www.inforegio.cec.eu.int/urban/upp/SRC/frame1.htm)

New information technologies provide, according to Manuel Castells, "fundamental means by which places may continue to exist as such ..... (through) the symbolic marking of places, the preservation of symbols of recognition, the expression of collective memory in actual practices of communication" (Castells, 1991) One interesting pilot project exploring the potential of such a neighbourhood-based IT strategy, focussed on cultural diversity, is Birmingham's Mediahub and Maverick Productions' web and live animation project,*Aston Pride*. The latter differs from other website initiatives in that it initiated a social process of face-to-face intergenerational and intercultural exchange, facilitated by the cultural animateurs of Sister Tree theatre company.

Jonnie Turpie, Maverick's director was the facilitator who helped the participants put themselves, and their streets, on the website, with photographs, views of life and perceptions of the 'others' in the project. He highlights the potential for extending connectedness and access through learning centres in libraries, schools, elderly people's homes, and through live screenings at community events such as the one *Aston Pride* held at Aston Villa Football Club, with media professionals and cultural animateurs collaborating with local marginalised and culturally diverse groups to facilitate self-representation and cross-cultural communication, for example by creating an interactive local TV channel. The potential for participation via e.democracy and straw polling, for example over ideas for Millennium Point, could be exploited to redress low levels of citizen involvement in decision-making. The website gives a glimpse of how photographs of streets and landmarks 'then and now', can tap memory and fantasy, both to enhance place identity and reconceive the future. Such a forward-looking memory bank and popular archive could create an imaginative resource for city planning and urban strategies. (www. mediahub.co.uk/ourstory/ourstories/ourstories.htm; Jonnie Turpie, interview with Jude Bloomfield, 23.12.01.)

Countering Ethnic Segregation in Public Life

a. Desegregating education: *Flemish Flying Colours*
Another approach to countering ethnic segregation is through strategies designed to address ethnic exclusion. There is no easy way to reverse market trends which conspire with individual aspirations and upward mobility to exacerbate ethnic segregation and marginalisation. Nowhere is this more evident than in schooling where the Government's policy of encouraging separate faith schools is perpetuating ethnic, as well as religious segregation of children, and if not, division, at least mutual ignorance.

One educational initiative which has succeeded in reversing this process is the Flemish Flying Colours project. Established as a pilot scheme five years ago in twenty five primary schools in Flanders and Brussels, it drew on the Chicago experience of art magnet schools which, like Apelarte, and other intercultural arts projects (Schlesischestrasse 27 in Berlin, London Diaspora City) use professional artists who work over a prolonged period of time with schools, to widen cultural opportunities for deprived children in neighbourhoods with a high concentration of new immigrants. They build up confidence and skills, valuing the diverse cultural experience and creativity of the children and also establish long-lasting two-way links with the communities which feed into the school art projects, which in turn, find their way back to the community through performances, exhibitions and concerts.

The project forms part of the official Belgian government framework for integrating immigrants. So the selection and training of the artists is organised centrally by the Flemish Centre for Amateur Art and Art Education and the outcomes are evaluated by the Centre for Intercultural Education in the University of Ghent. But it does not use art education simply as part of the school curriculum but to create a positive image of the school, the children and their cultural achievements in order to improve standing in the community. Photography and videos are deployed to picture the diversity of images of the community, and help reshape them positively. The photos are displayed locally in community centres and the videos shown on local television. (Bossuyt, Vlaggen en Wimpals, u.d.)

According to the evaluation after three years, the project has galvanised enthusiasm and commitment from the schools, children, staff and artists alike, that has spread to the local communities, so it has become 'an event' and encouraged positive responses to diversity "which was brought to the fore as an opportunity .... not viewed as a threat". Children's communication skills rapidly improved and the schools gained so much in popularity that they began to attract back children from white middle class areas. This then led to enhanced participation of parent committees in some schools. (Bossuyt, *With Flying Colours*, 17-18)

Clearly, this approach has only been implemented in primary, not secondary schools, and in a less prescribed school programme than exists in Britain with the rigidities of the National Curriculum. The government shelved the report by Ken Robinson on creativity in education and Flying Colours was a project he approved as head of the "Culture, Creativity and the Young" programme of the European Council. However, just as Tim Brighouse has found ways of introducing creative ideas into education, like the Learning Zone and Youth Parliament in Birmingham, it is hoped that cities can try out experiments of this kind which will begin to tackle ethnic segregation in schools.

b. Countering racism and exclusion in sport: *CARE*
Ethnic minority young people, especially Asian boys are deterred from participating in sports at competitive level – particularly football – due to racial harassment from fellow players, coaches and the overwhelmingly white public. This results in considerable hurt, psychological undermining and waste of their talent. It has the effect of discouraging Asians from attending matches, of making Asian boys withdraw from mixed teams, and either abandon the sport altogether or play for only Asian teams, as exemplified in the case of Sukhy Johal. He was the only Asian player in the Youth League in Nottingham from 1981-6 when he decided to withdraw owing to continuous racial abuse and played, from then on, only for all-Asian teams. (Sukhy Johal, interview with Franco Bianchini, 9.01.02.) This illustrates the detrimental effect of racism on the development of Asian footballers and helps to explain why there is currently no footballer from a British Asian background in the Premiership, and very few in the youth academies of Premier League clubs.

CARE - Charlton Athletic Race Equality Partnership – has undertaken a serious strategy for counteracting racism in football, by diversifying audiences and ensuring inter-ethnic support for the game. The club set up a partnership with its supporters, ethnic minority community groups, Greenwich Multi-Faith Forum, Greenwich council, University,

Woolwich College, Victim Support and the Metropolitan Police, with the aim of kicking racism out of the game and out of the area, and increasing the participation of ethnic minorities in the club. It has done this by offering half price tickets to members of the CARE forum and a tour of the ground to welcome members of the community groups who get tickets this way. CARE has put on a series of 'Red, White and Black' matches with other clubs, (playing on the club colours of red and white) to symbolise the commitment to ethnically mixed football, using for example, multicultural arts and cuisine at the Huddersfield match in 1998 to attract a broader crowd, and to alter the image of the club.

The longer term aim of preventing racist attitudes and behaviour setting in among young people, has been addressed through educational resource packs: 'Show Racism the Red Card' and 'Routes of Racism' disseminated through libraries and schools and for use by specially trained youth workers. Other educational initiatives have used multicultural art forms: such as a carnival arts workshop in five primary schools, a'Face Value' project for 10-16 year olds discussing prejudice, peer group pressure, racial violence and mixed race relationships, and the PATH summer project for 16-21 year olds which has used theatre and role-play, including performance workshops to explore friendship and difference and provide race equality training. (Policy Action Team 10, 1999, 100-102)

c. Addressing the isolation of immigrant women: *Alma Mater*, Turin

The Alma Mater Intercultural Women's Centre in Turin is an imaginative initiative which has transformed the traditional model of an immigrant welfare centre which treats migrants as clients and dependents, into a self-managed and intercultural social centre for women. Founded in 1993 by migrant women from Somalia, Morocco, the Ivory Coast and Iran, who worked primarily as domestics and care assistants in Italian people's homes, it addressed their own needs for a place to socialise, relax, and feel culturally at home, where they could be in charge. The centre experiments interculturally with food, health, recreation, education and training, attracting a lot of support from local feminists. It has developed ethnic cookery as a means of intercultural sharing and 'cultural enrichment', Turkish baths and Chinese massage as forms of bodily nourishment and intimacy denied in the outside society, and courses funded by the European Social Fund which trained a diverse group of 20 women as care assistants and a second group of 15 as cultural mediators – who organise cultural animation and festivals in their communities. (Interview with Sonia Amamiui and Enza Levaté, July 2003; www.women.it/impresadonna/associazioni/alm.htm www.women.it/impresadonna/progetto/ric_az.htm)

d. Diversifying the airwaves: *Radio Multikulti,* **Berlin,** *MATV,* **Leicester**
Public space is not just in streets and squares and in cyberspace but in the airwaves too. One notable example is Radio Multikulti, a public service broadcaster of SFB in Berlin, explicitly committed to building cultural respect for others and pluralising the public space of the airwaves. Johannes Thearer, the head of music, adopts a discourse on globalisation, seeking to reflect the multicultural reality which German law and culture construes as 'foreign', in all its plurality, without critical judgement. The channel is dedicated to world music, and set up the world music charts. It excludes only commercially dominant Anglo-American pop music from its programmes as an already over-exposed genre. It gives exposure to both traditional forms and innovative crossovers and has facilitated hybrids, issuing two CDs: 'African Beats' and 'Asian Beats'.

The limit of this initiative is that these are defined in traditional terms as though they derived from Africa or Asia rather than being a hybrid mix that came about in Berlin. In fact, they were the product of series of live concerts which Radio Multikulti put on, under the title – with no hint of post-modern irony - 'Drum and Tribe'. (Johannes Thearer, interview with Jude Bloomfield, 22.05.01.) It is significant that in Britain, world music has now begun to penetrate mainstream broadcasting, via BBC Radio 3, traditionally an exclusively classical music channel.

Another interesting development in terrestrial T.V. is marked by the first Asian-owned commercial stations in Britain, MATV in Leicester. This is available to all Leicester residents with a TV aerial. It presents news items from British Asian perspectives, as well as introducing non-Asian viewers to culturally specific art forms e.g. Bollywood films with subtitles, or classical Indian dance.

e. From Multicultural to Intercultural Festivals
The Leicester and Rotterdam Caribbean Carnivals
Festivals, Carnival and other community celebrations can both be associated with the cultural expressions of specific ethnic minorities

(or distinctive strands within them), and be civic celebrations belonging to the whole city. In a recent comparison of the Leicester and Rotterdam Caribbean carnivals, Pawlet Warner has highlighted the much greater ownership of Carnival in the Rotterdam case, facilitated by higher levels of municipal funding, greater involvement of the local media and businesses in promoting the event and its coherent integration into the city's public transport, tourism, place marketing, physical planning, economic development and education.

The Rotterdam Carnival is also more explicitly presented as an intercultural event, as a type of festival which has evolved and interacted with contemporary Dutch culture. British carnivals are also undoubtedly intercultural events, for example through the introduction of sound systems and floats on big lorries, which are specific British Jamaican innovations on the Trinidadian tradition which originally formed Carnival in Britain. However, the intercultural character of British Carnival is not perceived or communicated as such. On the contrary, the marketing of it often emphasises its 'ethnically exotic' character, thus freezing it in time and taking it back to its country of origin. (Interview with Pawlet Warner 21.12.01; Warner, 2002)

Karnivale der Kulturen (Carnival of Cultures), Berlin

Most cultural festivals in Britain do not represent the country's cultural diversity and are largely oblivious of this fact. So a cultural diversity audit of the programming and management of festivals is the first step towards realising their civic potential within a pluralistic public sphere. This is especially relevant to festivals which claim to be Birmingham-wide, or have Birmingham in their title, such as the Birmingham Writers and Readers and the Film and TV festivals. The inventions of new civic events can build on needs, desires and dreams, not to create a false sense of jollity or togetherness, (in some cases manufactured by tourist or place marketing agencies) but memorable festive occasions in which large swathes of the city participate in person, express their own ways of celebrating or commemorating, and share moments of conviviality. (See, Peattie in Douglass and Friedmann, 1998) Such occasions express the French urban theorist, Henri Lefevbre's idea of the *fête* as a disruption of established routines that prefigures a possible alternative future.

One example of an attempt at enacting a new pluralistic civic identity is the annual *Karnivale der Kulturen* in Berlin (which is not a Carnival in the African Caribbean, Latin American or Mediterranean sense which have their roots in Catholic culture) held in the streets, with participation of almost all the minority cultural organizations in the city, has become hugely popular, attended last year by an estimated 600,000 Berliners. However, the structure of the event is not fully intercultural. Hybrid forms of music are presented in traditional terms, according to country of origin, on separate stages – Turkish dance, Russian disco, reggae, tabla, and food stands are separated according to national, geopolitical or ethnic definitions of the culture (African, Latin American, Asian, Turkish, Indian) So while it succeeds in creating a multicultural public space, it does not recognise the full interculturality of the event by denying the cultural mixes that are a unique product of Berlin. (Bloomfield, 2001)

Creating an Intercultural Civic Identity and Culture

The objective of this strategy is to re-found the urban public sphere so that it reflects fully the cultural diversity and collective identity of the city.

Cultural diversity needs to be reflected in the symbolic and ceremonial spaces of the city centre, the 'front stages' as well as the backstreets and margins. Although there have been some experiments in specific localities where ethnic minorities are concentrated, these have not permeated into those spaces which symbolically represent the whole to its citizens, city users and to the outside world. This is not a question of counterposing the margins to the mainstream or ethnically distinctive districts to the city centre. It is rather an issue of ensuring that the diversity of the city as a whole is embodied in its public symbols e.g. rituals, celebrations and built environment.

a. Creating intercultural urban design: *Prasada* in Sparkhill
A promising experiment in intercultural design was carried out in the 'Balti zone' of the Ladypool Rd., Sparkhill in 1998, (funded partly by the ERDF's URBAN programme) by Prasada – a Sanskrit term for a temple or palace which is also an acronym for Practice, Research and Advancement in South Asian Design and Architecture. This institute was established as part of De Montfort University in Leicester in 1996. Prasada's aim was to bring together the study of traditional South Asian architectural forms, visual arts and crafts with contemporary South Asian cultural expression, primarily in Britain. The designs for the Balti zone project are based on Moghul motifs and forms which add to and interact with the Victorian pavilions and

church spires in the area. Designs for a pergola, market square, ornamental screening around a carpark, among others have not yet been implemented. (See illustrations) Consequently, the potential of this experiment can only be glimpsed through the street furniture – bollards, litter bins and street lighting - which has been installed. (Adam Hardy, Director of Prasada, interview with Jude Bloomfield, 21.12.01; *Prasada Newsletter* no. 3, autumn 1998)

The potential for this experiment in marrying traditional and contemporary South Asian design to create a new hybrid architecture in the public sphere has been curtailed by the decision of the University to close Prasada down. Thus the opportunity to develop a pioneering intercultural centre in Leicester has been lost, but the spirit of the project to translate traditional South Asian aesthetic forms into a modern idiom that reshapes the contemporary urban environment remains.

b. Information Technology at the service of Intercultural Communication Strategies: *Aston Pride*, Birmingham
Plans for extending access to information technology with digital link-ups across cities appear to offer great possibilities for cultural diversity strategies connecting marginalized groups to the society, enhancing participation and 'e.democracy'. It is easy to be mesmerised by the technology into thinking that in itself it will build up the cultural capital of information-poor people. There are numerous projects which have incorporated IT access into broader regeneration schemes such as the Gate in Turin, (see below) or are running limited experiments to test out specific social effects such as Telematic Naples. This is setting up telematic recreation centres in two squares in contrasting areas, one city-centre based with an ageing and declining population, the other in the eastern periphery of Ponticelli, with a young population, plus a network of telematic kiosks providing free information about city services, traffic and cultural events and also commercial listings. So the project is designed to facilitate generational access to communication technologies, rather than addressing cultural diversity as such.
(www.inforegio.cec.eu.int/urban/upp/SRC/frame1. htm)

New information technologies provide, according to Manuel Castells, "fundamental means by which places may continue to exist as such.... (through) the symbolic marking of places, the preservation of symbols of recognition, the expression of collective memory in actual practices of communication". (Castells, 1991) One interesting pilot project exploring the potential of such a neighbourhood-based IT strategy, focussed on cultural diversity, is Birmingham's Mediahub and Maverick Productions' web and live animation project, Aston Pride. The latter differs from other website initiatives in that it initiated a social process of face-to-face intergenerational and intercultural exchange, facilitated by the cultural animateurs of Sister Tree theatre company.

Jonnie Turpie, Maverick's director was the facilitator who helped the participants - put themselves, and their streets on the website, with photographs, views of life and perceptions of the 'others' in the project. He highlights the potential for extending connectedness and access through learning centres in libraries, schools, elderly people's homes, and through live screenings at community events such as the one Aston Pride held at Aston Villa Football Club, with media professionals and cultural animateurs collaborating with local marginalised and culturally diverse groups to facilitate self-representation and cross-cultural communication, for example by creating an interactive local TV channel. The potential for participation via e.democracy and straw polling, for example over ideas for Millennium Point, could be exploited to redress low levels of citizen involvement in decision-making. The website gives a glimpse of how photographs of streets and landmarks 'then and now', can tap memory and fantasy, both to enhance place identity and reconceive the future. Such a forward-looking memory bank and popular archive could create an imaginative resource for city planning and urban strategies. (www.mediahub.co.uk/ourstory/ourstories/ourstories.htm; Jonnie Turpie interview with Jude Bloomfield, 23.12.01)

c. Creating Symbolic Gateways and Quarters of the City: *the Gate, Turin*
Certain sites or quarters of a city play a symbolic role, embodying an essential quality, virtue or myth of the city – for example Paris's Left Bank symbolising its intellectual caché, or London's East End – danger, waste and vice but also rags to riches fortune. In regeneration strategies, therefore, the symbolic importance of a district to the city's overall self-image and character has to be taken into account. A skilful example of integrated regeneration in a quarter which played a symbolically negative role is the Gate project in Turin.

Surrounding the Piazza della Repubblica, it is one of the largest markets in Europe with over 1,000 traders with more than 200 stalls and shops, visited daily by up to 40,000 people. It acts as a meeting point for foreign and local residents, and at weekends, the lively market and frequent antique fairs, attract visitors from all over the city. It is also located near significant cultural heritage - the cathedral with the Chapel of the Sindone and the Roman Porte Palatine and has traditionally been the point of entry to the city for migrants, from the south, and now from outside the EU. Despite the evidence of its historical centrality, its fortunes have declined with the uncontrolled growth of traffic, pollution, social marginalisation, drugs and crime.

The Gate project has taken a bold and innovative approach to these problems resisting the gentrification and 'whitewashing' of the area by displacing immigrants and other low-income residents and 'undesirables'. An alternative to sanitising the neighbourhood by removal of the fruit and vegetable market has been applied through an environmental strategy, including incentives to residents to refurbish their houses and energy-saving schemes. The market's organic waste is to be recycled as compost for the local food growers and suppliers -- the Tuscan hill farmers - and in addition, a quality standard for fruit and vegetables introduced to upgrade the produce, and attract new customers.

The central objectives of the project are: firstly, to give back the Porta Palazzo neighbourhood to the whole city, by making it safer and more accessible through public transport, signage, pedestrianisation, electronic communication and linkages with schools, thus reinstating it as a civic gateway and symbol which its physical and historical centrality merits.

Secondly the aim is to improve the quality of life of local residents, market traders and users of the area, for example reducing the dependence of immigrant workers on criminal organisations, by setting up a recreational centre and advice and care centres, addressing the social and health problems – such as addiction and unemployment - of immigrants. The renovation of the shopping areas is also designed to reinvigorate the second-hand and antiques market, and enable regular antique fairs to take place which will attract visitors back to the area.

In the process, the project will have generated around 1,000 jobs, mainly on the renovation of housing in the market area and the construction of an underpass below the market. The support for small and medium-sized enterprises (SMEs) and the environmental pilot projects will also create employment and lead to around a 100 permanent jobs for young immigrants on the accompanying training and job placement schemes. (Cardia, 1999)

d. Intercultural Animation and 'Urban theatre'
Teatro dell'angolo's *Il gioco di Romeo e Giulietta* (*Romeo and Juliet's Game*)
Teatro dell'angolo, a Turin-based theatre company founded at the end of the 1960s as a co-operative, was born from the idea of actors as improvisers of social reality. It has become one of the eighteen nationally recognised 'Innovative Repertory Theatres for Children and Young People'. From its contemporary reinterpretation of classical myths like Ulysses and Robinson Crusoe, Teatro dell'angolo began to introduce the culturally diverse world around it into its stories, such as a black Cinderella. (*Cenerentola o della differenza*; Cinderella or speaking of difference)

In 2000, the theatre produced an extraordinary version of Romeo and Juliet – *Il gioco di Romeo e Giulietta*, that won the Grinzane Cavour prize – for encouraging young people to read. It was performed in the huge market square of Porta Palazzo in Turin – a densely populated immigrant quarter and emblematic gateway to the city where the Gate project is situated. The company worked for several months with hundreds of the young people in African drumming, dance and movement workshops in schools – and then selected fifty who rehearsed intensively for a month.

They dramatised the conflict between the Montague and Capulet families as a kind of interethnic gang warfare, in which the protagonists are caught on opposite sides of the fence, symbolised by a high net they get caught up in as they caress and kiss through the gap. It used the imagery of the market, the rich diversity of fruit and vegetables as symbols of human diversity, with the violence dissipated in smashing water melons. It was performed at night, with hundreds of lanterns, African drum and Arab music to the appreciation of the public of the area who saw their own lives reflected in the story. (Graziano Melano, interview with Jude Bloomfield, 9.7.03; video *Il gioco di Romeo e Giulietta*) This kind of collaboration turned the city into a stage and the performance enacted a new way of living together.

Teatro di nascosto – refugee Theatre of the Hidden, Volterra, Tuscany

The refugee theatre, Teatro di nascosto in Volterra, grew out of Annet Henneman's training and work in prison theatre with Armando Punzo. There they drew on the innate storytelling and performance skills of prisoners, who had no experience of theatre at all, and on dialect theatre, Neapolitan songs and hard physical training, insisting the prisoners had to 'be better than normal actors'. (Annett Henneman, interview with Jude Bloomfield, 26.7.03)

After seven years collaboration, Henneman decided she had to use her art to tell the world about the refugee crisis and injustice, through a theatre of reportage which would give voice to people who 'have no voice' and prevent the public consoling itself that the stories were just invented. So in 1998 she set up Teatro di nascosto with Gianni Calastri and a team of Italian actors, based primarily around the plight of the Kurdish people.

The methodology involved gathering material from the countries refugees had fled and building characters from the real life-stories. They visited Diyarbakir and Istanbul and on their return put on a *serata curda* (a Kurdish evening) set in a refugee camp in which the public heard some of the refugee stories, performed by Nascosto actors and then share a Kurdish meal and glass of tea. *Lontano dal Kurdistan/Ji Kurdistan durem* (Far from Kurdistan) was a follow-up on the experience of cruelty and torture, escape and the mixed emotions of exile, which mixed witness accounts, with photographs, songs and dance, that premièred at the festival in Pontedera in 1999.

The second major production *Sebri Eyub/La pazienza di Giobbe* (The Patience of Job) focussed on Iranian Kurdistan, following a visit to Kermanshah, Islam Abat and Tehran, where the actors were prevented from entering Iraq. The play dealt with the desperate waiting and blocked aspirations of exiles in Iran waiting to go to Europe or to find their families in Iraq, and included a Kurdish actor who had joined the company, Adil Yalcin. Other productions followed including monologues *Hedye, Payman and Ismail*. In 2001, they expanded their theme to world poverty, the underlying situation generating refugees with *La Scala della povertà* (The scale of poverty) combining stories gathered from the homeless sleeping rough outside Rome central station, with those from Calcutta and Kurdistan.

The training for theatre of reportage involves the actors in entering another culture. So they lived with three girls hidden in an apartment in Istanbul whose parents had escaped to Europe. In Turkish Kurdistan they met women whose sons had been eaten by dogs before their eyes. They became schooled in Muslim culture and the strong feelings for friendship that are not openly expressed. It became the actors' work to imitate the behaviour of the culture around them and in the process they learnt the Arabic language and Kurdish dancing with months of meticulous practice.

It was perhaps only one step further from this method acting to have actual refugees as players. So Henneman set up an academy with a three-year theatre training for asylum seekers and refugees, to train them to enact their own stories. Ten students from Africa, Afghanistan and Kurdistan were selected for the first intake. They lived together with Teatro di Nascosto in a living cultural exchange of traditions, languages and religions, sharing the psychological burdens of uncertain status and ongoing terror as well as formal learning of Italian, English and computer skills, to equip them to work as intercultural mediators.

The academy has confronted serious financial and political obstacles because of the Bossi Fini law, which closed down the national asylum programme (PNA) removing board and lodging allowance from asylum rejects. Nevertheless, the theatre has continued to work, producing and performing the show *Dinieghi*, (Refusals) based on the students' own stories of exile and asylum rejection, with the voice of the Committee deciding their fate offstage, with the performers on stage answering questions in their own language simultaneously, interspersed with songs and dance performed by a Rwandan dancer. So effective was the performance in the vast expanse of Milan station in 2002 that Médicins sans Frontières, Amnesty and ICS Network who saw the performance invited them to participate in their international campaign 'Right to Asylum – a civic question'. They have bought 40 performances to be staged over three years in theatres, schools, conferences, public squares and stations.

This international recognition affords the theatre a lifeline –although it survives on a shoestring combining the Amnesty funding with European funding for the Academy under the Equal Integra programme for integration which it has jointly with Teatro Ponte d'Era, sales and modest amounts from the Tuscan region which recognised Teatro di nascosto from its inception as one of its first Intercultural

Centres, he province and the city council. (Annet Henneman, interview with Jude Bloomfield, 27.7.03)

e. Setting up Centres for Intercultural Production and Performance: *Werkstatt der Kulturen,* Berlin

Cities need to create intercultural centres for projects of cultural production, bringing together people and organisations from diverse backgrounds, to sustain and give public visibility and support to projects which would otherwise struggle to get off the ground or be condemned to marginality. The *Werkstatt der Kulturen* - Workshop of Cultures – is such a space – a shared production and performance venue in Berlin, which organises the *Karnivale*. It has a concert hall, auditorium, laboratories and studios, run jointly by representatives of German and migrant organisations for young people. (Vertovec, 1995) It considers itself "a centre of the intercultural scene in Berlin" and facilitates cross-cultural collaboration. It operates an open-door policy to artists from the 'local international population', and organises training courses in a wide range of arts and media, workshops, discussions and conferences. However it still considers the artists and intellectuals of different nationalities as 'ambassadors of their culture', revealing that it is still affected by the German national designation of them as foreigners. ("Unser Auftrag", *Extra Top Berlin International,* Interview Andreas Freudenberg, 24.04.01;Werkstatt der Kulturen/SFB Radio Multikulti, September 1997, 64) An indication of the failure of the city authorities to embrace the project as a expression of Berlin's identity is its location in the peripheral district of Neu Kölln.

f. Reshaping Collective Memory to Include the 'Other'

Collective memory expresses attachment to the city and affection for it, but memory is selectively shaped by personal and group experience, scholarly and media accounts, museum exhibitions and displays, symbols embodied in monuments, sculpture and architectural heritage, as well as story-telling and anecdotes, songs, sayings, slogans and photographs. Generally the claims of indigenous memory triumphs over that of outsiders and newcomers, especially for countries with a colonial past. This makes the kind of intercultural, intergenerational projects for building local plural civic identity and public spheres so important.

Key to the solution to the problem lies in reconnecting the presence of outsiders and newcomers to the imperial/colonial history of the city and its industrial development that drew the labour force to it from previous colonial and underdeveloped parts of the world. Then the history of their coming, their own history of subordination, impoverishment or exile becomes part of the history of the city. The public symbols need to reflect on this double history, the symbolic statuary of the city centre can be challenged not only through pluralistic additions to imperial and monarchic statues but by juxtaposing symbols, through montage and parody, performing art and installations which interact with and comment on the lop-sided history. Likewise museums' collections can be contextualised to account for how its 'treasures' were acquired - through exploration, war and appropriation.

The Horniman Museum, London

The Horniman Museum in South London has begun a journey of revising its collection, as part of its £13.4 million redevelopment which will showcase its collection of world cultures. It has already opened a new African Worlds Gallery which explores mainly African masks and fascinating cross-cultural altars from Haiti, Benin and Brazil. The exhibition refers to local African immigrants and informants who donated objects or told stories and anecdotes about the rituals associated with the masks. It is also accompanied by an artist-in-residence programme 'My Africa Your Africa' which includes installations reflecting on the display and a series of workshops in the museum and with schools.

The museum also owns an ancient collection of musical instruments from all over the world and runs a World Music workshop for children, as well as a range of music appreciation courses for adults. So it is catering for a diversity of tastes, and in this sense is pluralistic. Nevertheless, what is remarkably absent from this anthropological approach, is a critical, historical sense of how the collection was acquired, and its link to the Horniman fortune which was derived from trading that most English of imperial acquisitions, tea. A serious inclusive curatorial policy for the museum cannot remain silent on the routes by which commodities arrived here and have come to be markers of Englishness. Likewise, the criteria of selection by which artefacts become objects in the museum's collection also need to be made clear. An intercultural approach to collective memory cannot select items to present African cultures as though they were unified, traditional, unchanging and thereby, exotic.

The *Haus der Kulturen der Welt*, Berlin

By contrast, the *Haus der Kulturen der Welt* (House of Cultures of the World) in Berlin, which operated on similar lines, has begun to make a culture shift from presenting the Third World as essentially 'primitive' and outside history, to recognising its own modernisation movements, resistance to colonialism and self-generated cultural and political avant-gardes. This can be seen from two exhibitions – one in 1997 entitled "*Die anderen Modernen*" - the Other Moderns - with 30 contemporary artists from Africa, Asia and Latin America and a series of debates problematising the supremacy of Western art, and the other "*The Short Century*", held last year on independence and liberation movements in Africa 1945-1994 which included politically inspired art, murals and posters of resistance like Kay Hasan's Flight, photography of the schizophrenic planning pressures on African cities, montages juxtaposing commercial motifs and traditional symbols, traditional forms like wood cuts, textiles and fabric figures, modern sculpture and installations assembling the débris of a life and diaries interweaving personal biography with historical change as in the film biopics of Fritz Fanon by Isaac Julien and Patrice Lumumba by Raol Peck. (Haus der Kulturen der Welt, 1999; 2001a; 2001)

The *Rich Mix Centre*, London's East End

The Rich Mix Centre in London has been explicitly set up to create intercultural understanding and inclusiveness, by celebrating and promoting London's cosmopolitan diversity and heritage. Strategically located in the Spitalfields area of London's East End, the gateway for immigrants to the city, it has converted an old disused industrial building into a multi-media, multi-purpose centre, combining traditional and futurist elements in its architecture and form with an internet café, digital museum and information centre, as well as food, craft and design halls, cultural industry workspaces and studios, performances space, audio-visual theatre and cinema, musical rehearsal rooms and recording studios and gallery with educational resources room attached.

The 'Virtual Reality' hall in the digital museum uses interactive modern technologies of sound and image to build on previous projects on the diversity of Londoners "*Exploring living Memory*" promoted by the GLC, "*Peopling London*" at the Museum of London and the Commission for Racial Equality's "*Roots of the Future*" and access a digital archive of multicultural experience. It will be important for the intercultural programme to develop critical historical perspectives and not just rely on the celebratory and experiential

approach of family histories and photographs, or be overwhelmed by the commercial drive to promote and market ethnically diverse cultural products, artefacts and tastes so as to neglect wider social and political dimensions.
(London Borough of Tower Hamlets c.1996; www.richmix.org.uk/r.proj.html)

g. Shaping Collective Self-Image through a Public Art Strategy: *Wide City*, Milan
Public art symbolises who the citizens of a city are, what events have made them, where they come from, which spaces they can inhabit, where they can go. (Miles, 1997) There are very few European examples which embody an intercultural understanding of the identity of citizens, where the history embodied in its images is diverse. However, a fascinating project in Milan, called Wide City, set up by the contemporary artist Luca Vitone, produced a cultural map of the city that linked up over 500 migrant cultural centres, foreign cultural organisations such as the Goethe Institute and British Council, cultural associations and projects, ethnic boutiques, delicatessens, book and record shops, take-aways and restaurants, community centres and holy places. This alternative itinerary of Milan revolved around a central exhibition, linked to weekly open days, with free buses taking people between the different cultural centres where visitors could get a taste of the different communities, their food, commercial activity, artwork, hear and see the work that goes on – widening their cultural experience of the city and opening up access to places they would not normally go. (Vitone, 1998)

h. Transforming mentalities
The Berlin Senate's *"Wer ist ein Berliner ?"* campaign
City governments are generally not accustomed to intervening in the nebulous field of public perceptions and consciousness which does not fit easily into the remit of existing departmental structures and professional division of labour. However, extending and pluralising involvement in the public sphere entails creating a welcoming and open civic culture which embraces others, is curious and exploratory, willing to experiment and try out what is unfamiliar and different. Cities cannot disengage from public perceptions which shape the quality of civic life, but should take up the task with flair and commitment. An imaginative public policy intervention of this kind has been undertaken by the Berlin Senate Commissioner for Foreign Affairs, aimed at changing perceptions of civic identity as unquestioningly monocultural, through a public survey and poster

campaign *Wer ist ein Berliner?* about what the diverse population of Berlin thought it meant to be a Berliner. The campaign was revived in November 2000 with the production of a 'Culture Bag' – shopping bag with the wide variety of views of Berlin identity printed on it. (Vertovec, 1995; Barbara John, Interview with Jude Bloomfield, 27.04.01; Bloomfield 2001)

Porto Franco Intercultura project, Tuscany

City governments are generally not accustomed to intervening in the nebulous field of public perceptions, which does not fit easily into the remit of existing departmental structures and professional responsibilities. However, extending and pluralising involvement in the public sphere needs a welcoming and open civic mentality, which embraces others and is willing to experiment.

The Porto Franco Intercultura project of the Tuscany region, in central Italy, represents a highly articulated intervention of this kind. It seeks to change perceptions of cultural diversity of visible minorities by recasting Tuscan identity as diverse, reinterpreting the history of Tuscany as the product of intercultural influences from the Etruscans to the Middle Ages, when Tuscan society was influenced by Arab traditions of science, philosophy and the arts. Porto Franco ("Free Port") argues that Tuscany is intercultural also by virtue of its location as a border region, where the Appenines separate Continental from Mediterranean Europe. By conceiving intercultural fusion as a general cultural process, Porto Franco seeks to normalise contemporary cultural diversity as a Tuscan tradition and to re-conceive contact and 'contamination' with others as a natural process of cultural change.

The project has initiated a network of 80 intercultural centres throughout the region from 1999 to 2001, utilising existing cultural organisations and civic institutions such as the Fabbrica Europa arts festival, Green and women's centres, and the local tradition of libraries as centres of intercultural learning. It developed integrated educational, training, social and cultural programmes with the centres and links with schools, cultural and social institutions. A series of five Summer University 'Campuses' were held in 2000 on the themes of women, writing, history and memory, culture of habitats, and religious cultures, extending to eleven throughout the spring and summer of 2001 on themes of history, resistance and memory. Allied to the project are intercultural publications - the first was on migration to Tuscany from 1000 to the present day by Lisa Francovich, issued in 1999 - a web newspaper and programme of conferences and debates, involving international figures such as Noam Chomsky, Rigoberta Menciù and Eduardo Galeano.

Perhaps the most important sign of the political commitment to, and investment in, this project "to govern the complexity of multiculturalism" (Zoppi, 1999) is the change to the administrative statute of the region to make interculturalism an integral part of its practice and educational, social and cultural policies with funding mechanisms adjusted accordingly (the project's budget rose sixfold from 1999 to 2000 to £600,000).

(See www.cultura.toscana.it/intercultura.htm and Porto Franco, Toscana. Terra dei popoli e delle culture: i documenti del progetto, 1998-2001, www.cultura.toscana.it/progetti/porto franco/home.htm)

Conclusions

1. Rethinking Political Representation Interculturally: from 'the community' to the 'local public sphere'

Cities need to establish a collaborative relationship with ethnic minorities which can address those issues of discrimination, demonisation, and criminalisation – such as racial violence, police harassment and higher levels of unemployment and school exclusions, as Birmingham's Stephen Lawrence Commission of Inquiry and the Partnership Group emerging from it have begun to do. A direct forum with ethnic minorities can contribute to creating a context for mutual social learning, helping culturally diverse groups become aware of different and conflicting needs and aspirations, to work out their priorities and develop strategic capacities. On the other side, it offers city authorities the possibility of ongoing dialogue, input and feedback, helping it to keep in touch with creative and imaginative ideas. Such a process can produce constructive solutions.

a. Inter-ethnic and inter-faith forums: *The Black Londoners' Forum*

This organisation grew out of the London Civic Forum, which was set up with statutory rights under the Greater London Authority (GLA) to express the diversity of London's civil society, lobby on its behalf and consult with and brief the citizens. The Black Londoners' Forum has a consultative relationship with the mayor and the new Greater London Assembly, advising them on issues of special concern to ethnic minorities in the city. It organises the collective voice of ethnic minorities through its network which has currently reached almost 1,000 organisations. Through the *Reconnecting London* project, funded through the Single Regeneration Budget, this network is being extended to the far reaches of the marginalised, by involving elderly disabled, unorganised black young people and more specialised organisations like the North London Muslim Housing Association.

The Forum organises policy forums around issues concerning business, the arts, youth, the voluntary sector and faith, through which it formulates policy and lobbies relevant statutory bodies – such as the police, the London Development Agency as well as the city authority. An example of how it is revitalising local democracy by channelling an ethnic minority voice, is its input to the London Strategic Plan. It held a public debate involving culturally diverse communities and black professionals from the Society of Black

Architects and the Association of Black Planners in preparation of its briefing to the GLA.

Another issue it has begun to raise which acutely affects its business members is contractualisation. It has not yet developed a policy forum on the public sector which is also deeply affected by this, and employs large numbers of ethnic minorities as service workers. The Forum is growing rapidly and reinventing itself as it goes, like the London Civic Forum. The latter is considering moving over to representation on the basis of communities of interest rather than functional sectors. It is heartening to see culturally diverse organisations being open to experiment in this way with political forms and networks.

b. Spreading Civic Competencies: *Operation Black Vote*
Cities can facilitate this kind of initiative in collective self-organisation by providing training in civic competencies – such as accessing the local media, applying for grants, bringing ideas to fruition in projects for the city. There are rare but outstanding examples of independent initiatives of this kind, such as Operation Black Vote (OBV, 1997) in London which tours schools and ethnic minority organisations encouraging black participation in politics at all levels and has initiated mentoring schemes where young people from ethnic minorities shadow MPs, councillors, magistrates and school governors to remove the mystique of power, by showing the workings of the institutions and the nature of the job. This approach aims to build self-confidence at an individual level, and could be extended to building confidence in collective organisation, by training in campaigning skills and media representation.

2. Rethinking City Practices

a. Crossing administrative and funding divides
The Porto Franco example raises the question sharply of the change in mentality and practice which an intercultural approach calls for within the administrative structures of city and regional authorities so that they are able to generate pluralistic ways of thinking and working in their own organisation. Some of the issues that we have become aware of are the need to:

- **revise administrative mechanisms across old departmental divides** to facilitate brainstorming and problem-solving. The conversations it needs to ensure take place must tap the reserves of talent and ideas within the city and regional authority's own organisation and with partners throughout the diverse civil society.

- **combine funding streams imaginatively** so that they can integrate different dimensions of cultural diversity – such as integrating training with culturally sensitive health provision or educational programmes and workshops with Carnival. Improving evaluation enhances advocacy which helps to secure more continuity in funding.

b.   Openness to Ideas and Social Innovation
Cities often do not admit mistakes and so cannot engage in a creative process of social learning. Huddersfield's *Creative Town Initiative* (Landry, 2000, 79-87), in the local authority's efforts to respond to industrial decline, developed a strategy for opening up its policy-making system to outside ideas and initiatives – through such mechanisms as the Creativity Forum and Create! which sought to bring together creative thinkers in the town. Hothouse Units were set up to bring innovative businesses together through discussion salons, the setting up of *Brass*, a magazine of Northern creativity, a website and a shared database of creative projects. (Landry, 2000, 80-1.)

This strategy aimed to reposition the town in inter-urban competition and in the international division of labour, 'unleashing talent and harnessing intellectual capital' and, within that, cultural diversity, for the regeneration of the town. This kind of openness has not been generalised or adopted forcibly elsewhere. For the city to become intercultural and socially creative openness to ideas and initiatives and interactivity with civil society need to become embedded in policy-making.

For an intercultural mentality to take root, long term investment is needed: investment of time to experiment, take risks, and learn from failures; patience is required for sensitive ethnographic research, building trust with culturally diverse people who may have good reason to be suspicious or hostile to the authorities; intercultural training and literacy are essential requisites to understanding and interpreting reluctance and silence; political will is necessary to stay the course even if there are few short-term visible and exploitable gains to show. Nor is such an intercultural mentality confined to

ethnic minorities, but is shared by other marginalised and disadvantaged groups and social movements.
Some of the measures cities can take to develop a capacity for social learning and intercultural thinking are by:

- **creating a memory bank and narrative of urban innovation.** A number of important cultural diversity initiatives cited here came from Birmingham. Yet we found no account of these achievements or of the cultural shift in the city's thinking on any of the best practice websites. By contrast, Metro Toronto promotes itself as an innovator in this field, winning acclaim for thinking through cultural diversity across all its services. Even more important than telling the story to the outside world, is creating a memory bank and archive of creative practices in cultural diversity which is easily accessible and widely popularised through the press, city marketing, promotion and tourism.

- **critical reflection and creative relationship to social movements.** In the large-scale redevelopment of Birmingham city centre, popular campaigns were mounted with the involvement of community activists and critical planners in response to attempts to demolish landmarks (see, for example, Green Ban Action's efforts to save the Victorian Post Office in Chamberlain Square). The Birmingham for People pressure group campaigned against repeating planning errors of constructing more subways and corporate blocks without a street plan in the Bull Ring redevelopment. In both cases, the city showed a lack of critical reflection and wasted the imaginative resources of these movements. which had formulated serious alternative plans. City authorities need to listen to their social critics and learn from their mistakes, so they can be creatively absorbed and lead to improved policy-making processes.

- **soliciting public debate and ideas.** The city can engage in creative debate on policy priorities by initiating and responding to debates on letters pages of the local press, by genuine research consultation with local groups, – for example of young black people who feel excluded from public spaces in the city centre – where their feelings are listened to and proposals actively sought. Groups whose views and experience are not usually tapped into in the design of policies and planning for their needs, are not confined to ethnic minorities. An intercultural approach would also embrace the diversity of needs of women, children, the disabled, the elderly, gay and lesbian people. Suggestion boxes for children but also more discursive forms of participation that discuss ideas and solutions – through the kind of intergenerational - as well as intercultural - communication project undertaken by Aston Pride, could be far more widely applied, including young and elderly people, and people of widely different cultural backgrounds in debates about the local 'commons'. The city council should encourage these forms of participation and integrate these sources of ideas into its policy-making.

c. Rebuilding Research Capacity and a Creative Relationship with Universities

The financial crisis in local government in Britain and other European countries, has led to a cut in research capacity, as well as in planning and maintenance services. Little is known or researched about ethnic minority social and economic networks and creative forces, such as who the gatekeepers of the networks are, what is the up-and-coming talent, what are the links between diasporic networks and the local economy, how such networks connect to the informal economy. The roles of dealmakers and brokers, 'the movers and shakers' and of ethnic minority entrepreneurship are vital to developing an alternative globalisation to that centred on the South East, which is the only truly internationally competitive city region. (See Amin, Massey, Thrift, 2002) To revitalise cities with ethnic minority populations in Northern England and the Midlands, and mobilise the creative potential of cultural diversity to regenerating their economies, city authorities have to grow in-house research capacity. Contracting out research cannot fully solve the problem because of the danger that the research will not be well-managed or its findings integrated into policy-making.

The potential for embedding creativity and intercultural innovation lies in the 'third sector' – of socially managed and integrated small firms - which requires strong regional and local urban policy initiatives, on training, shared premises in knowledge communities, soft loans, investment support and technical services. Although regional development agencies make great play of commitment to creativity, they, like local authorities, are under great pressure to look for the quick fix and sure winners, and risk neglecting the sometimes painful development of small-scale cultural businesses and self-employed cultural producers. However, this is where intercultural innovation, employment and economic growth tends to take place.

Cities can capitalise on the creative potential of cultural diversity by:

- **forming a more creative relationship with the academic community**. Some of the most interesting initiatives cited here have come out of qualitatively new relationships with sociologists, anthropologists and historians – in terms of intercultural literacy, subtlety and social depth. For example, the Apelarte project was directed by Cristina Santhinho, an academic anthropologist who went to work full-time for Loures council, whereas the Porto Franco project grew out of links with anthropologists, cultural organisers and the libraries movement in Tuscany. It is important that politicians and policy-makers respond openly to social research findings, and apply them creatively to policy, seeing research as an opportunity for more finely-tuned intervention and longer term success in making the city an intercultural and cosmopolitan place.

- **overcoming gaps in knowledge**. It is important that the city addresses the gaps in knowledge, particularly about the relationship between social, cultural and financial capital in ethnic minority networks; the links between the international and local economy through diasporic financial and trade flows; the productivity of sub-cultural networks and deficits in training, skills and services; the sources of migrant entrepreneurialism and the obstacles that are faced. If the city can propose a research agenda and manage this kind of intercultural research in partnership with the university, it will develop its internal research capacity for intercultural policy-making. At the same time, it will help embed intercultural research in the university. Both these will contribute to making the city intercultural in its mentality and policy thinking, and so diffuse interculturalism in all aspects of urban life.

INTERVIEWS

Unless otherwise indicated, these interviews have been carried out by Jude Bloomfield.

Alma Mater Intercultural Women's Centre, Turin, Sonia Amamiui, Enza Levaté, 7.03.

Cynthia Bower, Assistant Director Social Services and chair of Northfield Constituency Action Team, (now Director, South Birmingham Primary Healthcare Trust), 22.12.01.

Anna Ferrero, Director, Intercultural Centre, Turin, 7.03.

Andreas Freudenberg, Director Werkstatt der Kulturen, 24.4.01.

Modou Gueye, Senagalese actor and Chair of Maschere Nere theatre, Milan, 8.7.03.

Adam Hardy, Director of Prasada, Leicester, 21.12.01.

Helmut Hartmann, multicultural programmer at WUK, Vienna, 1.7.03.

Annett Henneman, Director of Teatro di Nascosto – refugee Theatre of the Hidden, London, 26.7.03.

Hugo Hinsley, Lecturer at Architectural Association, on Spitalfields, London, 12.12.01.

Sukhy Johal, former Asian footballer, interviewed by Franco Bianchini, Leicester, 9.1.02.

Barbara John, Commissioner for Foreigner Affairs, Berlin Senat, Berlin, 27.4.01.

Kanak Attak: Imran Ayata, Dagmar Ganssloser, Minu HascheniMichael Wittenbücher, Berlin, 29.5.01.

Tela Laeo, consultant international cultural co-operation, Lisbon, 13.7.03.

Graziano Melano, Director Teatro dell'angolo, Turin, 9.7.03.

Venod Mitra, Ambitious Productions, Chocolate Factory, Haringey, North London.

Celena Nair, Black Londoners' Forum, Londoon, 14.12.01.

Pascal Nicolas, Director Cultural Centre, Berchem, Antwerp 19.6.03.

Gianguido Palombo, cultural consultant/writer on international cultural co-operation and interculturalism, Rome, 7.7.03.

Darryl Telles, London Civic Forum, London, 14.12.01.

Johannes Thearer, Head of Music on Radio Multi-Kulti, Berlin, 22.5.01.

Michael Thoss, Director, Haus der Kulturen der Welt, Berlin, 28.5.01.

Jonnie Turpie, Maverick Television Company, Birmingham, 23.12.01.

Pawlet Warner on Caribbean Carnivas in Rotterdam and Leicester, Leicester, 21.12.01.

REFERENCES

Ahmed Nafeez Mosaddeq, Bodi Faisal, Kazim Raza and Shadjareh Massoud *The Oldham Riots Discrimination, Deprivation and Communal Tension in the United Kingdom*, Media Monitors Network, 2001 at:
www.mediamonitors.net/mosaddeq6.html

Albrow M. in Eade J. Ed. *Living in the Global City: Globalisation as Local Process*, London: Routledge, 1997.

Alibhai-Brown Yasmin, *True Colours. Public Attitudes to Multiculturalism and the Role of Government*, IPPR, 1999.

Alibhai-Brown Y. *Who Do We Think We Are? Imagining the New Britain*, Penguin, 2000.

Alibhai-Brown, Y. *Beyond Multiculturalism*. London, Foreign Policy Centre. Foreign Policy Centre, 2001.

Amendola, G. ed. Culture and Neighbourhoods. Volume 4: Perspectives and Keywords, Strasbourg: Council of Europe Press, 1998.

Amin A. *Ethnicity and the Multicultural City*, Report for the Dept. of Transport, Local Government and the Regions and the ESRC Cities Initiative, January 2002.

Amin A. and Thrift N. *Cities. Reimagining the Urban,* Cambridge: Polity Press, 2002.

Amin A., Massey D. and Thrift N., *Decentring the Nation*, London: Catalyst, 2003.

Appadurai A. 'Disjuncture and Difference in the Global Cultural Economy', in Featherstone M. ed. *Global Culture, Nationalism, Globalisation and Modernity*, 1990.

Audrey S. *Multiculturalism in Practice: Irish, Jewish, Italian and Pakistani Migration to Scotland*, Aldershot: Ashgate, 2000.

Aulakh P. and Schechter M. eds. *Rethinking Globalisation (s) From Corporate Transnationalism to Local Interventions,* London: Macmillan, 1998.

Banting, Kymlicka, Crick et.al "Too Diverse? Replies to David Goodhart's essay" *Prospect,* March 2004.

Baumann G. *Contesting Culture,* Cambridge: Cambridge University Press, 1996.

Baumann G. 'Dominant and Demotic Discourses of Culture: their Relevance to Multi-Ethnic Alliances', in Werbner P. and Modood T. eds. *Debating Cultural Hybridity* Zed Books, 1997.

Beauregard R. and Body-Gendrot S. *The Urban Moment. Cosmopolitan Essays on the late 20th Century City,* Thousand Oaks/London/New Dehli, Sage, 1999.

Bennett T. *Differing Diversities. Cultural Policy and Cultural Diversity,* Strasbourg: Council of Europe publishing, 2001.

Bianchini F. with Santacatterina L.. *Culture and Neighbouthoods. Volume 2: A Comparative Report,* Strasbourg: Council of Europe Press, 1997.

Birmingham Specialist Community Health NHS Trust, *Raising Diversity Awareness,* submission to the British Diversity Awards, 2001.

Birmingham Stephen Lawrence Inquiry Commission *Challenges for the Future: Race Equality in Birmingham,* Birmingham: Birmingham City Council, 2001.

Black Londoners' Forum, *Black London,* Issue 2, November 2001.

BLF, 'For the Black Minority Ethnic Community on the Greater London Authority's Spatial Development Strategy', 2001.

Bloomfield J. and Bianchini F. 'Cultural Citizenship and Urban Governance in Western Europe' in Stevenson N. ed. *Cultural Citizenship,* London: Sage, 2001.

Bloomfield J. "'Made in Berlin' Multicultural Conceptual Confusion and Intercultural Reality", *Journal of International Cultural Policy*, October 2003.

Bloomfield J. *Crossing the Rainbow: Multicultural and Intercultural Performing Arts in Europe*, IETM: http://www.ietm.org/, October, 2003.

Borja J. and Castells M. *Local and Global: Management of Cities in the Information Age*, Earthscan, 1997.

Bossuyt T. *With Flying Colours*, VCA Booklets, Flemish Centre for Amateur Arts and Art Education, Brussels, undated c.1999.

Bourdieu P. *Outline of a Theory of Practice*, Cambridge: Cambridge University Press, 1977.

Bourdieu P. *Distinction: a Social Critique of the Judgement of Taste*, London: Routledge and Kegan Paul, 1984.

Brown I.M. *Inclusion and Democracy*, Oxford University Press, 2000.

Brubaker R. W. *Citizenship and Nationhood in France and Germany*, 1992.

Brubaker R.W. ed. *Immigration and the Politics of Citizenship in Europe and North America*, Lanham, MD: University Press of America, 1989.

Calhoun C. ed. *Social Theory and the Politics of Identity*, Oxford: Blackwell, 1994.

Cantle T., *Community Cohesion: A Report of the Independent Review Team*, Home Office, 2001.

Cardia L. "Un progetto per Porta Palazzo", 1999 www.a-torino.com/progetti/thegate.htm

Carley M. *et.al. Regeneration in the 21st Century*, London: Policy Press and Joseph Rowntree Foundation, 2000.

Castells M. *The Informational City*, Oxford: Blackwell, 1989.

Castro, R. *Civilisation urbaine ou barbarie*, Paris: Pion, 1994.

Cohen P. "From the Other Side of the Tracks: Dual Cities, Third Spaces, and the Urban Uncanny in Contemporary Discourses of 'Race' and 'Class'", in G. Bridge and S. Watson ed., Companion to the City, Blackwell, 2000, 316-330.

Commission on the Future of Multi-Ethnic Britain, *The Parekh Report:The Future of Multi-ethnic Britain*, Runnymede Trust, Profile Books, 2002.

Department for Culture, Media and Sport, *Policy Action Team 10. A Report to the Social Exclusion Unit*, London: DCMS, 1999.

Derrida J. *On Cosmopolitanism and Forgiveness*. London: Routledge, 2001.

Douglass M. and Friedmann J. eds. *Cities for Citizens*, Chichester: John Wiley, 1998.

Eade J. Ed. *Living in the Global City: Globalisation as Local Process*, Routledge, 1997.

Entzinger H. "A Future for the Dutch 'Ethnic Minorities' Model?", in Lewis B. and Schnapper D. eds., *Muslims in Europe*, London/N.Y.: Pinter, 1994, pp. 19-38.

Fainstein S. 'Can we make the cities we want?', in Beauregard R. and Body-Gendrot S. *The Urban Moment. Cosmopolitan Esays on the late 20th Century City*, Thousand Oaks/London/New Dehli, Sage, 1999.

Faist T. "Transnationalization in international migration: implications for the study of citizenship and culture", *Racial and Ethnic Studies*, 23, 2000, 189-222.

Favell A. *Philosophies of Integration: Immigration and the Idea of Citizenship in France and Britain*, Macmillan, 1998.
Favell A. "Italy as a Comparative Case" in Grillo R. and Pratt J. eds. *The Politics of Recognizing Difference: Multiculturalism Italian –Style*, Aldershot/Burlington USA: Ashgate, 2002.

Featherstone M. and Lash S. eds. *Spaces of Culture: City –Nation-War.*, Sage 1999.

Ferrero A. ed. *Corpi Individuali e Contesti Interculturali*, Turin: L'Harmattan Italia, 2002.

Finlayson A. "Elements of the Blairite Image of Leadership", *Parliamentary Affairs*; 55, 2002; 586-599.

Friedman J. "Being in the World: Globalisation and Localisation" in Featherstone M. ed. *Global Culture, Nationalism, Globalisation and Modernity*, Sage 1990.

Friedman J. 'The Hybridisation of Roots and the Abhorrence of the Bush', in Featherstone M. and Lash S. eds. *Spaces of Culture: City – Nation-War.*, Sage 1999

Gaspard F. Khosrow-Khavar F. *Le Foulard Et La République*, Paris:La Découverte, 1995.

Gold, S.J. Transnational Communities: Examining Migration in a globally integrated world in Aulakh P. and Schechter M. eds. *Rethinking Globalisation (s) From Corporate Transnationalism to Local Interventions.*

Goodhart D. "Too Diverse?" *Prospect*, February 2004.

Graham S. and Marvin S. *Telecommunications and the City*, London: Routledge, 1996.

Greenhalgh L. and Worpole K. *Park Life. Urban Parks and Social Renewal*, London: Comedia in association with Demos, 1995.

Habermas J 'Struggles for Recognition in the Democratic Constitutional State', in Taylor C. et al., Gutman A. ed. *Multiculturalism: Examining the Politics of Recognition*, Princeton New Jersey: Princeton University Press, 1994.

Hailbronner K. "Citizenship and Nationhood in Germany" in Brubaker R.W. ed. *Immigration and the Politics of Citizenship in Europe and North America*, Lanham, MD: University Press of America, 1989.

Hall S. 'Cultural Identity and Diaspora', in J. Rutherford ed. *Identity, Community, Culture and Difference*, Lawrence and Wishart, 1990.

Hall S. 'New Ethnicities' in Donald J. and Rattansi A. eds. *"Race", Culture and Difference*, London: Sage, 1992.

Hall S. 'Who Needs Identity?' in Hall S. and Du Gay P. eds. *Questions of Identity*, London: Sage, 1996.

Hall S. and Du Gay P. eds. *Questions of Cultural Identity*, London: Sage, 1996.

Hamnett "Social Polarisation, Economic Restructuring and Welfare State Regimes", *Urban Studies*, 33, 1966, 1407-30.

Haus der Kulturen der Welt, *1989 bis 1999*, 1999.

Haus der Kulturen der Welt, *Tasks and Goals*, 2001a.

Haus der Kulturen der Welt, *The Short Century*, 2001b.

Hellman J. "Immigrant 'Space' in Italy: When an emigrant sending becomes an immigrant receiving society," *Modern Italy*, vol.2, number 1/2, autumn 1997.

Holton R.J. 'Multiculural Citizenship' in Isin E.F.ed. *Democracy, Citizenship and the Global City*, London and New York: Routledge, 2000.

Houari C., Hadj N.and Thomas W., *J'y suis resté depuis/En daar ben ik gebleven*, DitoDito/EPO/Le Cactus/La Boutique Culturelle, September 2000.

Isin E.F.ed. *Democracy, Citizenship and the Global City*, London and New York: Routledge, 2000.

Isin E.F. and Wood P.K. *Citizenship and Identity*, London, Thousand Oaks, New Dehli: Sage,1999.

Kahn V. Home Ownership in the Inner City: Salvation or Despair?, Aldershot: Gower, 1985.

Kalb D, van der Land M., Staring R., van Steenbergen B and Wilterdink N. eds. *The Ends of Globalisation. Bringing Society back in,* Lanham: Rowman and Littlefield Publishers, 2000.

Kelly P. 'Contractarian Social Justice' in Boucher D. and Kelly P. eds. *Social Justice: From Hume to Walzer,* Routledge, 1998.

Kelso P. and Vasagar J. Guardian Special Report on Muslims in Britain "Muslims reject image of separate society", *The Guardian,* 17.06.02.

Kennedy P. and Roudometof V., *Communities across Borders. New Immigrants and Transnational Cultures,* Routledge, 2000.

Kastoryano R. and Crowley J. Multicultural Policies and Modes of Citizenship: France, Paris city profile, UNESCO-MOST Multicultural Policies and Modes of Citizenship in European Cities templates: mirror.eschina.bnu.edu.cn/Mirror2/ unesco/www.unesco.org/most/p97city.htm.

Khakee A., Somma P. and Thomas H. eds. *Urban Renewal, Ethnicity and Social Exclusion in Europe,* Aldershot: Ashgate, 1999.

King R, Fielding A. and Black R. "The International Migration Turnaround in Southern Europe", in King R. and Black R. eds. *Southern Europe and the New Migration,* Brighton: Sussex Academic Press, 1997.

Kontos M. "Biographic" or "ethnic" resources? The missing dimension of motivation in understanding ethnic business "Paper presented at the international conference" Biographical Methods and Professional Practice". The Open University,Tavistock Centre, London19–21 October 2000.
Kvistad G. "Membership without Politics? The Social and Political Rights of Foreigners in Germany" in Kurthen H., Fijalkowski and Wagner G. eds. *Immigration, Citizenship and the Welfare State in Germany and the United States: Welfare Policies and Immigrants' Citizenship,* Stamford Connecticut/London: Jai Press Inc., 1998.

Kundnani A. "From Oldham to Bradford: the violence of the violated" in The Three Faces of British Racism. A Special Report, *Race and Class,* vol. 43.no.2, October-December 2001.

Landry C. *et al. The Art of Regeneration*, Bournes Green: Comedia, 1996.

Landry C. *The Creative City*. A toolkit for Urban Innovators, London: Comedia with Earthscan Publications, 2000.

London Borough of Tower Hamlets and its Partners, *The 'Rich Mix Centre' for London*, Submission to the Millennium Commission, c.1996.

Lucassen J. and Penninx R. Newcomers: Immigrants and their Descendants in the Netherlands 1550-1995, Amsterdam: HetSpinhuis, 1997.

Maan B. *The New Scots: The Story of Asians in Scotland*, Edinburgh: John Donald Publishers, 1992.

Malik K., "The Real Value of Diversity", *Connections*, winter 2002.

Miles M. Art, Space and the City. Public Art and Urban Futures, London: Routledge, 1997.

Miles R. "The Articulation of Racism and Nationalism: Reflections on European History" in Solomos and Wrench, eds. *Racism and Migration in Western Europe* (Berg, 1993).

Morén-Alegret R. *Integration and Resistance. The relation of social organisations, global capital, governments and international immigration in Spain and Portugal*, Aldershot: Ashgate, 2002.

Nicolas P. 'Flanders, 'Cultural Diversity at Multiple Speeds', translation for Congress on Multicultural Theatre in Europe, Amsterdam (NL), April 25-26 2001 of Biebauw K and Nicolas P. 'Culturele diversiteit op de politieke agenda: hoop en wanhoop' in *Zwarte Schapen, Wite Raven, Cahier Culturele Diversiteit*, nr 1 Hoofdstuk 27, 2001.

Operation Black Vote, *Preparing for the Future*, Biennial Report, 2000.

Parekh B. *The Parekh Report: The Future of Multi-Ethnic Britain*, Runnymede Trust, Profile Books, 2002.

Parekh B. 'Reconstituting the modern state' in Anderson J. ed. *Transnational Democracy. Political Spaces and Border Crossings*, 2002.

Peach C. *The Caribbean in Europe: Contrasting Patterns of Migration and Settlement in Britain, France and the Netherlands*, CRER, September 1991.

Phillips T. Interview, *The Times*, 4.04.04.

Phillips T. Speech at the Civil Service Race equality Network Annual Lecture, 26.04.04.

Portes, A. *Globalization from Below: The Rise of Transnational Communities*. Oxfore ESRC Transnational Communities Programme, September 1997.

Portes A. ed. *The Economic Sociology of Migration. Essays on Networks, Ethnicity and Entrepreneurship* New York: Sage, 1995.

Porto Franco, Toscana. *Terra dei popoli e delle culture: i documenti del progetto, 1998-2001*, pdf documentation:
www.cultura.toscana.it/progetti/porto_franco/home.htm
Rogers A. 'Citizenship, Multiculturalism and the European City' in Bridge G. and Watson S. eds. *A Companion to the City*, Blackwell 2000.

Rogers A. and Tillie J. Multicultural Policies and Modes of Citizenship in European Cities, Ashgate, 2001.

Sandercock L. *Towards Cosmopolis*, Chichester: John Wiley, 1998.

Sandercock L. *Cosmopolis II: Mongrel Cities in the 21st Century*, London/New York: Continuum, 2003.

Santhinho C. "*Pilot project 'Apelarte' Education and Multi-cultural policy'*" paper to Conference "Cities and Regions; Cultural Diversity – a Precondition for a United Europe", Innsbruck, 10th-11th December 2000.

Santos De Sousa B. 'Toward a Multicultural Conception of Human Rights' in Featherstone M. and Lash S. eds. *Spaces of Culture: City – Nation-War.*, Sage 1999.

Santos De Sousa B. *Towards a New Common Sense: Law, Science and Politics*, Routledge, 1995.

Sibley D. *Geographies of Exclusion*, London/New York: Routledge, 1995.

Stalker P. *A No Nonsense Guide to International Migration*, London: Verso, 2001.

Smith S. "Residential segregation: a geography of English racism?" in Jackson P. ed. *Race and Racism: Essays in Social Geography*, London: Allen and Unwin, 1987.

Soysal Y. *Limits of Citizenship. Migrants and Postnational Membership in Europe*, Chicago: U.P., 1994.

Soysal Y. 'Boundaries and Identity: Immigrants in Europe', *EUI Working Papers*, 96/3, 1996.

Spencer R.G. *British Immigration Policy since 1939*, London and New York: Routledge, 1997.
Terracciano A. "South Asian Diaspora Theatre in Britain", 2002, www.tara-arts.com

Thornton S. *Club Cultures: Music, Media and Subcultural Capital*, Cambridge: Polity, 1995.

Tomlinson J., *Globalisation and Culture,* Cambridge: Polity, 1999.

Turner B.S. 'Cosmopolitan Virtue' in Isin E.F.ed. *Democracy, Citizenship and the Global City*, London and New York: Routledge, 2000.

Van Amersfoort H. and Doomernik J. 'Emergent Diaspora or Immigrant Communities? Turkish migrants in Netherlands', in Eade J. Ed. *Living in the Global City: Globalisation as Local Process*, London: Routledge, 1997.

Vermeulen H. and Penninx R. eds. *Immigrant Integration: The Dutch Case*, Amsterdam: Het Spinhuis, 2000.

Vertovec S. "Berlin Multikulti: Germany, 'Foreigners' and 'World-Openness'", *New Community*, 22 (3), 1995.

Vertovec S and Peach C. eds. *Islam in Europe; The Politics of Religion and Community*, Macmillan 1997.

Vertovec S. and Rogers A. *Muslim European Youth. Reproducing ethnicity, religion and culture*, Aldershot:Ashgate, 1998.

Vitone L. *Wide City*, Comune di Milano, Progetto Giovani, 1999.

Wallman S. *The Diversity of Diversity: Implications of the Form and Process of Localised Urban Systems*, Fondazione ENI Enrico Mattei Working Paper series, KNOW 76. 2003 available at: www.feem.it/Feem/Pub/Publications/WPapers/default.html

Warner P. "A Study of Caribbean Carnivals in Leicester and Rotterdam" unpublished paper, M.A. in European Cultural Planning, De Montfort Unviersity, Leicester, June 2002.
Watson S. and Gibson K. eds. *Postmodern Cities and Spaces*, Oxford: Blackwell, 1994.

Werbner P. and Madood T. eds. *Debating Hybridity*, London/New Jersey: Zed Books, 1997.

Young I.M. *Inclusion and Democracy*, Oxford: Oxford U.P. 2000.

Yuval-Davis N. 'Citizenship, territoriality and the gendered construction of difference', in Isin E.F.ed. *Democracy, Citizenship and the Global City*, London and New York: Routledge, 2000.

Zoppi M. *Porto Franco Turin, Intercultura una nozione*, Il Manifesto di Porto Franco, May 1999: www.cultura.toscana.it/progetti/porto_franco/home.htm

WEBSITE REFERENCES

Alma Mater Intercultural Women's Centre Turin:
www.women.it/impresadonna/associazioni/alm.htm
www.women.it/impresadonna/progetto/ric_az.htm

Aston Pride:
www.mediahub.co.uk/ourstory/ourstories/ourstories.htm

Barcelona's Forum 2004:
www.barcelona2004.org

Birmingham City Council website:
www.birmingham.gov.uk/text/GenerateContent?CONTENT_ITEM_ID
=8475andCONTENT_ITEM_TYPE=0andMENU_ID=11028;

LGIB Projects and Partnerships Team Priority Countries:
www.lgib.gov.uk/intcoop/south_africa.htm

Flemish Flying Colours project:
Vlaggen en Wimpals //users.pandora.be/c.v.a/

The Gate, Turin www.a-torino.com/progetti/thegate.htm
www.inforegio.cec.eu.int/urban/upp/SRC/frame1.htm

Hyson Green, Nottingham:
www.life-at-the-heart.co.uk/hyson.htm

Kanak Attak manifesto at:
www.passagiere.de/ka/manifest/Manif_en.htm

Metro Toronto on European Good Practice Information Service
(EGPIS):
www.cities21.com/egpis/

Porto Franco Intercultura, Tuscany:
www.cultura.toscana.it/intercultura.htm
www.cultura.toscana.it/progetti/porto_franco/home.htm

Rich Mix Intercultural Centre, London:
www.richmix.org.uk/r.proj.html

Spitalfields Market, Brick Lane:
www.eastendlife.com/crt/fun_bricklane.shtml
www.smut.org.uk/

Undervaerket, Randers, Denmark:
www.undervaerket.dk/;
www.inforegio.cec.eu.int/urban/upp/SRC/frame1.htm

ADDITIONAL WEB RESOURCES

Crossing Brussels:
http//brussels2000.vub.ac.be/crossing/nl/page1.html
Erasmus 2001, Rotterdam:
www.erasmus2001.nl/

The Authors

Jude Bloomfield is an independent researcher on urban cultures, planning and citizenship, a translator and poet. She has taught, modern German - Italian - and comparative European - politics, cultural policy and history at a number of different universities including University College London, University of East London and De Montfort University, Leicester where she is currently a research associate of the International Cultural Planning and Policy Unit. She is a collaborator with Comedia, currently as a researcher on the Comedia, Rowntree funded *The Intercultural City: Making the Most of Diversity*, project. Her most recent publications are *Crossing the Rainbow*, (www.ietm.org, October 2003) a study of the multicultural and intercultural performing arts in nine European countries and " 'Made in Berlin' Multicultural Conceptual Confusion and Intercultural Reality", *Journal of International Cultural Policy*, October 2003.

Dr Franco Bianchini is Reader in Cultural Planning and Policy, Director of the International Cultural Planning and Policy Unit, and course leader for the MA in European Cultural Planning at De Montfort University, Leicester. He is also an Associate of Comedia, with whom he has collaborated since 1987. He has acted as advisor and researcher on cultural planning strategies and projects to many cities, arts councils and European institutions, including the Arts Council of England, the Council of Europe, the European Commission and the European Task Force on Culture and Development. His books include *Culture and Neighbourhoods: A Comparative Report* (with L.Ghilardi, Santacatterina, Strasbourg, Council of Europe,1997), *The Creative City* (with C. Landry, London 1995), *Cultural Policy and Urban Regeneration: the West European Experience* (with M. Parkinson, Manchester University Press, 1993). He co-authored "Cultural Citizenship and Urban Governance in Western Europe" with Jude Bloomfield in *Culture and Citizenship*, (Stevenson N. ed., Sage, 2001).